FAULT LINES &
TECTONIC PLATES

Discover
What Happens
When the
Earth's Crust
Moves

with **25** Projects

Kathleen M. Reilly

Illustrated by Chad Thompson

~ More earth and space science titles in the *Build It Yourself* Series ~

Check out more titles at www.nomadpress.net

Nomad Press
A division of Nomad Communications
10 9 8 7 6 5 4 3 2 1

This book was manufactured by CGB Printers,
North Mankato, Minnesota, United States
January 2017, Job #216316
ISBN Softcover: 978-1-61930-465-9
ISBN Hardcover: 978-1-61930-461-1

Educational Consultant, Marla Conn

Questions regarding the ordering of this book should be addressed to
Nomad Press
2456 Christian St.
White River Junction, VT 05001
www.nomadpress.net

CONTENTS

PS

Interested in Primary Sources?

Look for this icon. Use a smartphone or tablet app to scan the QR code and explore more about plate tectonics! You can find a list of URLs on the Resources page.

If the QR code doesn't work, try searching the Internet with the Keyword Prompts to find other helpful sources.

plate tectonics 🔍

ABOUT 275 MILLION YEARS AGO

The supercontinent Pangaea is formed.

ABOUT 200 MILLION YEARS AGO

Pangaea begins breaking up.

ABOUT 150 MILLION YEARS AGO

China begins to attach to what is now Asia, while North America and Europe begin to break away.

ABOUT 130 MILLION YEARS AGO

North America and Europe break apart.

ABOUT 50 MILLION YEARS AGO

Australia breaks apart from Antarctica.

1912

German scientist Alfred Wegener proposes the continental drift theory, which he calls "continental displacement."

1950s

Ships and submarines map the ocean floor, discovering mid-ocean ridges that help support the idea of sea-floor spreading.

1936

Japanese seismologist Kiyoo Wadati writes a paper that proves the evidence of deep earthquakes. He also writes the first accurate description of the inclined zone of deep earthquakes.

1935

American seismologist Hugo Benioff first proposes that subduction zones cause earthquakes.

1931

Atlantis, the first ship specifically created to study marine biology, geology, and oceanography, is built.

1929

British geologist Arthur Holmes proposes a theory of convection that pushed continental drift.

1960

Harry Hess, an American geologist, proposes that sea-floor spreading is constantly adding new material to the ocean floor.

1961

American scientist Robert Dietz proposes the hypothesis that new crust material is formed at oceanic ridges and spreads outward by centimeters every year.

1963

British geologists Frederick Vine and Drummond Matthews use the discovery of magnetic striping of the ocean crust to support the idea that the planet's plates separate at mid-ocean ridges.

1965

Sir Edward Bullard, a British geologist, shows that the continents fit better together along their continental shelf areas rather than along the current coastlines.

1968

The *Glomar Challenger* is built. It is the first research ship that drills samples of rock in the deep ocean floor, offering evidence of sea-floor spreading.

SEPTEMBER 2016

Kent Condie, a geochemist at the New Mexico Institute of Mining and Technology, announces tectonic activity is increasing. He and his colleagues say the rate has doubled over the last 2 billion years.

AUGUST 2016

Inspired by the deadly earthquake and tsunami that hit the Indian Ocean in December 2004, a team of international researchers return to offshore Sumatra to collect marine sediments, rocks, and fluids.

DISCOVER PLATE TECTONICS!

PUZZLE

Did you know that the surface of planet Earth is similar to one enormous jigsaw puzzle? A puzzle is made up of anywhere from a few pieces to thousands of pieces. And each piece has a very specific shape that allows it to fit perfectly against another piece of the puzzle, right?

Take a close look at the shape of the continents on our planet. If you study them very carefully, you'll see that they kind of look like puzzle pieces. Look at the shape of Africa. See how the west coast of Africa curves inward? Now look at the shape of South America. What do you notice about the east coast of that continent?

WORDS TO KNOW

plate tectonics: the theory that describes how plates in the earth's crust slowly move and interact with each other to produce earthquakes, volcanoes, and mountains.

plates: huge, moving sections of the earth's crust.

tectonic: relating to the earth's crust and the forces acting on it.

theory: an idea or set of ideas intended to explain something.

fault line: a fracture in the earth's crust. Major fault lines form the boundaries between the tectonic plates.

Pangaea: a huge supercontinent that existed about 200 million years ago. It contained all the land on Earth.

perforations: dented lines where something can be easily broken or torn away from the rest of an object.

What if you were assembling a puzzle and saw two pieces like Africa and South America? Would you try to fit them together?

A German scientist named Alfred Wegener noticed this back in 1912. He started thinking, "What if these two continents actually *had* been one piece, but somehow broke apart?"

That question is what led to the study of **plate tectonics**. This is the idea that the surface of the earth is made of **plates**, or giant chunks of land, and that they are actually drifting extremely slowly over the surface of the earth. The **tectonic** plates are moving more slowly than you would ever be able to see just by watching.

PS

No Way!

When Alfred Wegener began to present his **theories** of plate tectonics to the scientific community in the early 1900s, he was laughed at, threatened, and criticized. The rest of the world wasn't ready to listen to his ideas, and he had no actual evidence to prove his theory. It wasn't until the 1960s, 30 years after Wegener died, that scientists discovered his theories were correct and the science of plate tectonics began to move forward. He is sometimes referred to as the "Copernicus of Geosciences." Can you figure out why? You can see pictures of him and look at his original notebooks, which are written in German, here.

Alfred Wegener Institute Copernicus 🔍

Major **fault lines** are the areas where the plates
bump against each other and pull apart.

ALL TOGETHER NOW!

Scientists believe that about 200 million years ago, the earth actually
had only one enormous landmass. All seven continents that we have
now were fused together into one giant continent called **Pangaea.**
This supercontinent had weak lines throughout it. Think of it as
a big graham cracker that has dents, or **perforations**, where you
snap it into smaller pieces.

When Pangaea began to break up, the giant
landmass split along these lines into plates. Each
plate now drifts super slowly, about 1 to 2 inches
per year, on the earth's surface. During the past
200 million years, the plates have drifted into the
positions the continents have today.

Fun Fact

Tectonic plates
move about
as fast as your
fingernails grow!

WORDS TO KNOW

continent: one of the earth's large landmasses, including Africa, Antarctica, Australia, North America, South America, and Asia and Europe.

In this book, we'll learn how the plates broke apart and moved away from each other. We'll also discover what impact these plates and the spaces between them have on the earth today.

You might not think something so huge that moves so slowly can have any effect on your daily life. But the movement of the plates is responsible for earthquakes, volcanoes, and other natural events, and even creates new landscapes. We'll learn how people are affected by the plates and their movement. Let's discover what's going on deep underground, far beneath your feet.

Good Science Practices

Every good scientist keeps a science journal! Scientists use the scientific method to keep their experiments organized. Choose a notebook to use as your science journal. As you read through this book and do the activities, keep track of your observations and record each step in a scientific method worksheet, like the one shown here.

Each chapter of this book begins with an essential question to help guide your exploration of tectonic plates. Keep the question in your mind as you read the chapter. At the end of each chapter, use your science journal to record your thoughts and answers.

Question: What are we trying to find out? What problem are we trying to solve?
Research: What do other people think?
Hypothesis/Prediction: What do we think the answer will be?
Equipment: What supplies are we using?
Method: What procedure are we following?
Results: What happened? Why?

? ESSENTIAL QUESTION

If you were a scientist, how would you try to prove your theory that the **continents** were once all together as one big continent?

Measure the Movement of Plates

You'll need to have a lot of patience for this project. If you stick with it, you'll have a great understanding of how the continents move! Ask an adult to help you find a location where it is safe and acceptable to use pins that will remain undisturbed for at least a month. You don't want to use a nice wall in the house!

For this project, you need a long area where you can put pins or tape that won't be disturbed. If you're using a wall, you'll want to start at the far end of one side. Other options include an outdoor tree or a series of branches or logs outside. If you're using masking tape, you can use the floor in a room of your house that doesn't get used.

Place a pin or piece of masking tape at the far end of your chosen location. If you're using tape, you can write the date on it. If you're using pins, just write down the date you start in your science journal.

The next day, come back to your location. Using your ruler or measuring tape, measure 1 inch away from your first location and place another pin or piece of tape. Come back the next day and do the same thing. You'll do this every day for one whole month!

At the end of the month, measure the distance from the very first mark to the last. How far away are they? How does this correspond to the number of days? Have a helper stand at the first marker, while you stand at the last. Does it look closer or farther than you thought?

THINK ABOUT IT: The plates of the planet move about 1 inch every year. How many years are represented by your entire project? Does that seem far for plates to move apart over that length of time? What If each inch of your project represented 10 years? How far would the plates have moved in that length of time? Try to figure out how far plates will move over your entire life. How far have they moved during your parents' lives?

ACTIVITY

5

Chapter 1

THE MOVEMENT OF TECTONIC PLATES

Have you ever watched chunks of ice float around on the top of your drink? These chunks of ice are similar to what the plates of the earth are like. The plates don't float around as freely as actual ice cubes or ice floes, but the huge land masses called continents aren't fixed in place. They move!

The plates don't move fast. It's not like we're all living on giant skateboards of land. They move at a rate you can't see or feel, about 1 inch every year. If you take a look at a ruler, you can see it's not far at all. Imagine moving that distance in a whole year! That's incredibly slow.

? ESSENTIAL QUESTION

What would the earth be like if it were still one giant continent? How would things be different? How would they be the same?

Think about adding that distance up, inch by inch, year by year. It's taken tens of millions of years for the plates to drift as far apart as they have. In another chapter, you'll learn how scientists figured out the plates were moving, even when they couldn't actually see or feel the movement. Let's take a closer look at what's going on under our feet.

ice floe: a large piece of ice that floats on water.

geologist: a scientist who studies geology, which is the history, structure, and origin of the earth.

inner core: the innermost layer of the earth, made of super-hot solid metal.

WORDS TO KNOW

LAYERS OF THE PLANET

Planet Earth isn't just one big chunk of rock, like an enormous marble floating in space. It's not hollow, either, like a soccer ball. Instead, **geologists** believe the earth is made up of layers.

Think about a peach—it has a stone pit in the center, then a soft, fleshy part that's juicy, and then the very thin skin that protects it all.

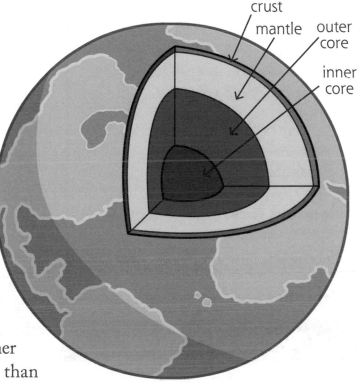

crust
mantle outer core
inner core

That's similar to the layers of the earth. First, there is an **inner core** made of solid metal. It's solid because of the intense pressure. The metal is so hot that it's almost as hot as the surface of the sun! This inner core is just a little smaller than the moon.

outer core: the layer of the earth surrounding the inner core, made of molten metal.

molten: melted by heat to a liquid.

mantle: the layer of the earth between the crust and core. The upper mantle, together with the crust, forms the lithosphere.

magma: hot, melted rock below the surface of the earth.

crust: the outer surface of the earth.

lithosphere: the rigid outer layer of the earth that includes the crust and the upper mantle.

sedimentary rock: rock formed from the compression of sediments, the remains of plants or animals, or from the evaporation of seawater.

sediment: bits of rock, sand, or dirt that have been carried to a place by water, wind, or a glacier.

fossil: the remains or traces of ancient plants or animals left in rock.

metamorphic rock: rock that has been transformed by heat or pressure or both into new rock, while staying solid.

pressure: a force that pushes on an object.

igneous rock: rock that forms from cooling magma.

lava: hot, melted rock that has risen to the surface of the earth.

basalt: a black, shiny volcanic rock.

WORDS TO KNOW

The next layer that surrounds the inner core is the **outer core**. This layer is not as hot but is made of **molten** metal, which is fluid instead of solid.

Surrounding the outer core layer is the **mantle**. This is the thickest part of the planet. While it's not as hot as the inner and outer cores, it's hot enough that the rocks in the mantle flow, like Silly Putty. The rocks are solid but weak, which allows them to flow. In some places the rock is partially melted and is called **magma**. The farther away from the core, the cooler and more solid the rock becomes.

The final layer of the earth is called the **crust**. This is the thinnest layer. The crust is solid and it's what we walk on.

WHERE DO WE STAND?

The earth's crust combined with the very top part of the mantle is called the **lithosphere**. This layer is what is divided up into the tectonic plates.

Scientists have identified seven or eight major plates on the planet, along with many smaller minor plates and micro plates, which are even smaller. The plates have names. The major plates are named the African, Antarctic, Eurasian, North American, South American, Pacific, and Indo-Australian Plates.

Fun Fact

The earth's crust isn't just the land we walk on. It covers the entire earth, even the bottom of the oceans.

Rocks Can Melt?

Although you can't simply toss a rock in the oven to melt it, rocks can melt into magma under extremely high heat. There are three main types of rocks on Earth. The different types are based on how they're formed.

› **Sedimentary rocks** are formed from bits of sand, pebbles, shells, and other bits of material, which is all called **sediment**. During the course of millions of years, layers of sediment harden into rock. You can identify sedimentary rock because it's fairly soft—for rock—and crumbles or breaks apart more easily than other kinds of rock. Sometimes you'll find **fossils** in sedimentary rock.

› **Metamorphic rocks** are rocks that are formed under the surface of the earth. They are created by intense heat and **pressure**. When you look at this type of rock, you might see shiny crystals that have formed from minerals that have grown slowly during the passage of time.

› **Igneous rocks** are the ones that are big players in plate tectonics. They're formed when magma cools and hardens. Sometimes this can take place inside the earth, and sometimes it takes place when the magma erupts from a volcano, in which case it's called **lava**. When that lava cools quickly, it creates igneous rocks. If you examine an igneous rock it might look shiny, as though it's made out of glass. Examples of igneous rock are granite, **basalt**, and obsidian. Basalt is studied by scientists to understand plate tectonics, as you'll learn later.

WORDS TO KNOW

converge: to come together.

magnitude: the measurement of the strength of an earthquake.

epicenter: the point on the earth's surface that is directly above the **focus** of an earthquake.

focus: the location of the source of an earthquake.

convection current: the movement of hot air or liquid rising and cold air or liquid sinking.

dense: when something is tightly packed in its space.

Some scientists consider the Indo-Australian Plate to be two separate plates, the Indian Plate and the Australian Plate. Although the plates have very similar names to the continents, each continent is not an actual plate. You have to picture the earth with all the oceans removed, and then draw lines to divide everything up into plates. That's because some of the plates' boundaries run along the crust at the bottom of the oceans. So while the edges of some plates do actually run along the borders of continents, other edges run deep under the ocean or through the middle of continents.

LET'S GET MOVING!

The plates don't just stay in the same place on the earth—they move. That's because the layer of the earth just below the lithosphere is the lower mantle, which is made of hot, flowing rocks.

The Pacific Plate

The Pacific Plate is under the largest ocean on Earth. The Pacific Ocean is an area where a few plates **converge**, including the Pacific Plate with the North American Plate, and the Nazca Plate with the South American Plate. This convergence creates zones that are home to large earthquakes. One of the largest recorded earthquakes, a **magnitude**-9.5 earthquake, had its **epicenter** where the Nazca and South American Plates converge.

The heat that radiates from the core of the earth is constant, like the heat on your stove. But it doesn't stay the same temperature everywhere. Instead, it's uneven, like the flames in a campfire—some spots are warmer than others.

Because of this uneven heat, the mantle rocks flow around instead of simply sitting still. Think of a pot of boiling noodles. The heat causes the noodles to move up and around the pot—if you watch steadily for a while, you'll see the noodles move in kind of a circular pattern. They'll rise up in the middle of the pot, where it's the hottest, and flow downward around the sides, where it's just a little cooler. This movement is called a **convection current**.

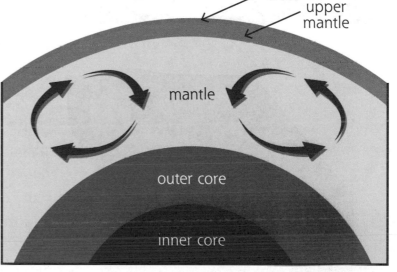

When rocks are so hot that they actually flow, the same movement happens. The solid rock in the earth's mantle flows in convection currents, all around the entire globe. Hotter solid mantle is less **dense** and flows up, while cooler solid mantle is more dense and sinks. As it moves, it pushes and pulls the tectonic plates along with it, making them move, too.

convergent boundary: where two plates come together, forming mountains and volcanoes and causing earthquakes.

subduction zone: where one tectonic plate slides under another tectonic plate.

divergent boundary: where two plates are moving in opposite directions and pulling apart, creating a rift zone. New crust forms at rift zones from the magma pushing through the crust.

rift zone: an area where the crust of the earth is pulled apart.

geyser: a hot spring under pressure that shoots boiling water into the air.

transform boundary: where two plates slide against each other.

WORDS TO KNOW

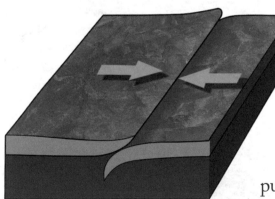

convergent boundary

RESPECT THE BOUNDARIES!

What happens to tectonic plates when they move? The areas where the plates meet each other are called boundaries. The way the plates move determines what happens at their boundaries and what that boundary is called. There are three types of boundaries: convergent, divergent, and transform.

Wherever any of these boundaries are, when the plates move, you'll feel it in the form of an earthquake. Afterward, the landscape might be changed dramatically and include volcanoes, trenches, and mountain ranges.

Convergent boundary: This type of boundary is where two plates push together, which pushes the edge of one or both plates up or down. This movement can create a mountain range as both plates push up like a steeple or, if one plate bends downward, the movement can form a trench in the ocean floor.

THE MOVEMENT OF TECTONIC PLATES

Volcanoes and earthquakes can occur along convergent boundaries. Scientists have found that ocean trenches, which are deep ravines in the ocean floor, form at convergent boundaries where one tectonic plate slides under another plate and sinks into the earth's mantle. This process is known as subduction and this kind of plate boundary is a **subduction zone**.

Divergent boundary: This type of boundary is formed where two tectonic plates are moving away from each other. Earthquakes can often happen along this type of boundary. In the space created between the plates, called a **rift zone**, magma rises up from the super-hot mantle beneath. **Geysers** often shoot superheated water from the gaps that are formed when the plates move away from each other.

Fun Fact

Tectonic comes from the Latin word *tectonicus*, which means "belonging to a building." In this case, the "building" is the structure of the earth!

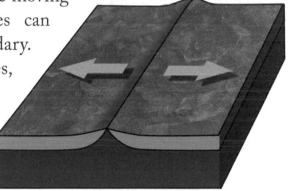

divergent boundary

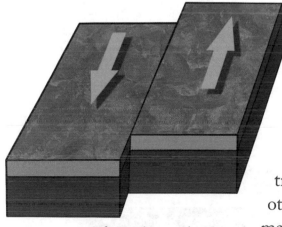

transform boundary

Transform boundary: This type of boundary happens when two plates slide past each other in opposite directions. The plates lurch and grind past each other, pulverizing rocks and destroying any human-made structure that might be built on top of the boundary. One thing that makes transform boundaries different from the other two types of boundaries is that no magma is released from the mantle below.

You won't find volcanoes along transform boundaries. Most transform faults are located in the ocean, but some of them form on land. The most notable is the famous San Andreas Fault that runs along the coast of California.

You can imagine how tough it must be for massive plates of rock to move past each other. It's not an easy glide. Instead, they push and strain against each other, getting stuck for periods of time. Then, when the pressure is so great they finally move, it's the sudden release of energy that causes earthquakes.

You can see the results of movement along transform boundaries.

The San Andreas Fault

When the San Andreas Fault had an earthquake in 1906 in San Francisco, the northern sections of the fault moved northward, and the result was clearly visible in the pattern of the earth afterward. The San Andreas Fault is one area that scientists are keeping a close eye on. The southern section is experiencing a strain that's been building up for more than 300 years. Some scientists believe the pressure is continuing to build in this section and that a large earthquake could be triggered at any time. You can see photographs of the city of San Francisco after the 1906 earthquake there. Can you see where the land buckled and twisted?

You can also read a letter written by someone who witnessed the earthquake.

San Francisco 1906 USGS

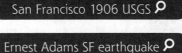

Ernest Adams SF earthquake

Fun Fact

The Mississippi River is what remains of a rift that formed in an ancient ocean around 1 billion years ago.

Imagine if you drew a picture of a stream on a piece of paper. Then, suppose you tore that paper in half, splitting your stream into two pieces right down the middle. Now, what if you put those pieces together again, but instead of lining them up so your stream looks like it did before, you slid the two pieces in opposite directions a little bit? That's what the land looks like after a transform fault experiences an earthquake and the pieces move in opposite directions. The land is misaligned.

BREAKING UP

The earth has gone through many changes since it was first formed. Scientists believe that the most recent dramatic change was the breakup of the single supercontinent of Pangaea.

Originally, Pangaea was surrounded by one enormous body of ocean water. Then, this single land mass began breaking up over a series of stages. Scientists believe the first stage of the breaking apart of Pangaea happened in the **Jurassic Period**, between 145 and 200 million years ago.

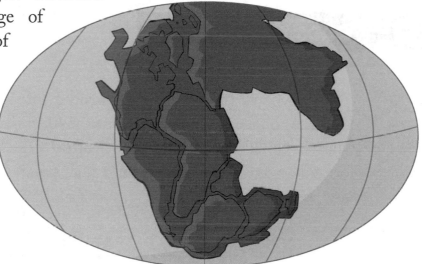

Pangaea Period

rift: an open space, such as where the crust of the earth is pulled apart.

Cretaceous Period: a period of time between 142 and 65 million years ago. This is when the earth was quite warm and sea levels were quite high. It is also when the dinosaurs disappeared.

landform: a physical feature of the earth's surface, such as a mountain or a valley.

seismic wave: the wave of energy that travels outward from an earthquake.

hotspot: a small area where hot magma rises, usually in the middle of a plate.

Paleocene Epoch: a period of time between 65 and 55 million years ago. This is when the mammals and birds **evolved** into many different forms.

evolve: to change or develop slowly, during long periods of time.

WORDS TO KNOW

The movement of the plates created a **rift** where the crust of the earth pulled apart. This massive rift occurred between the areas of land now known as the continents of Africa and North America. The rift formed a new ocean—the Atlantic Ocean.

On the other side of Africa, more rifts were occurring within the same time period. Eventually, these rifts formed the Indian Ocean.

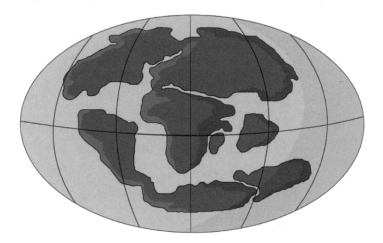

Cretaceous Period

The second stage of the breakup of Pangaea happened about 150 to 140 million years ago, during what is called the **Cretaceous Period**. The South Atlantic Ocean formed, and Madagascar and India separated from the continent now known as Antarctica.

India merged into Eurasia, and New Zealand moved away from Australia to become an island in the Pacific Ocean.

Mid-Atlantic Ridge

The movement of plates creates many different types of **landforms** along the boundaries. There is a long ridge in the middle of the floor of the Atlantic Ocean that marks the location of the divergent plate boundary. Plate movements here create earthquakes, but the earthquakes are smaller and don't impact humans as much as the Pacific Plate earthquakes can. Deep in the ocean, the earthquakes produce **seismic waves** and spew lava, but don't impact land very much.

The country of Iceland sits right on a **hotspot** of the Mid-Atlantic Ridge, which is why it has so many hot springs. In fact, the people of Iceland heat most of their homes using this water heated from deep within the earth, and even use it to keeps their roads and parking lots free of snow and ice in the winter.

The last major phase of Pangaea's break-up was about 65 to 55 million years ago, during the **Paleocene Epoch**. In this phase, Greenland broke free from Eurasia, creating the Norwegian Sea. The Atlantic and Indian Oceans kept expanding. India moved north and collided with Asia and Australia started its move from Antarctica.

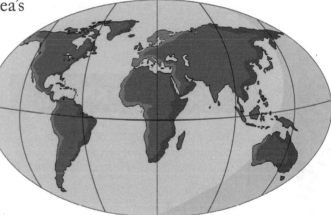

Palaeocene Epoch

?

ESSENTIAL QUESTION

Now it's time to consider and discuss the Essential Question:
What would the earth be like if it were still one giant continent? How would things be different? How would they be the same?

Evolution of the Planet

IDEAS FOR SUPPLIES
poster board ○ art supplies ○ clear plastic sheets

Our planet has evolved over time. The locations of the continents now are not where they used to be, and they're not the same shape they were in the past! With this project, you can create evolving maps that let you see where the continents have moved, how they've changed, and how different everything looks from the past. Use this website as a reference for your maps.

Geology Pangaea 🔍

Create a map of the earth with the equator and equally spaced lines of **latitude** and **longitude** stretching from the North Pole to the South Pole. Paint your map blue for the ocean and don't include the continents.

WORDS TO KNOW

latitude: imaginary lines around the earth that measure a position on the earth to the north or south of the equator.

longitude: imaginary lines running through the North and South Poles that indicate where you are on the globe.

Permian Period: a period of time between 290 and 248 million years ago. This is when all the continents came together into the supercontinent Pangaea.

Triassic Period: a period of time between 248 and 205 million years ago. This is when dinosaurs appeared.

Place one sheet of clear plastic over your map, lining it up carefully over the map. Using the earth maps you found as a guide, carefully draw the land masses of the earth on this first plastic sheet, creating the planet the way it looked when Pangaea was the big land mass, 250 million years ago in the **Permian Period**. This is map #1.

Repeat the drawing process with the land masses of earth the way they looked 210 million years ago, in the **Triassic Period**. This is map #2.

Repeat this process for the next three time periods:

* Map #3: 145 million years ago (Jurassic)
* Map #4: 65 million years ago (Cretaceous)
* Map #5: Present day

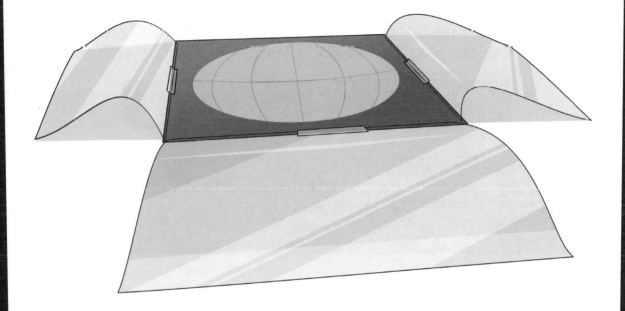

Arrange the clear maps on your world map and shift between them to see the differences between the time periods.

* How do the continents move around the equator?

* Where do you expect different land formations to develop?

THINK MORE: What are some other ways you can display the changing planet? Consider using a computer, modeling clay, other people, and anything else you can think of! How do your materials contribute to your understanding of plate tectonics?

Edible Molten Rock

1 cup sugar ○ ½ cup water ○ ½ cup light corn syrup
candy thermometer (optional) ○ red food coloring (optional)
cinnamon flavoring (optional) ○ plastic food gloves

It's difficult to comprehend how something as hard and solid as rock can actually melt. That takes a really high heat! Just as a candle can be solid, then melt into a liquid, then harden back into a solid, so can rock! This project will help you explore that idea.

Caution: You'll need an adult's help with this project. Be very careful with the boiling sugar syrup!

Apply a coating of nonstick spray to a baking sheet and set it aside. With an adult's help, mix together the sugar, water, and corn syrup in a saucepan.

Heat the mixture to boiling over medium-high heat. Be sure to stir it occasionally so the mixture doesn't burn or stick to the bottom of the saucepan. Once the mixture starts boiling, reduce the heat to medium, and stir it frequently.

If you have one, use a candy thermometer to measure the temperature, heating the mixture until it's 270 degrees Fahrenheit. If you're not using a candy thermometer, you can test the temperature by dropping a few drops of the syrup into very cold water. Once it separates into hard threads, it's the right temperature. You don't want to heat it more than that or you'll get brittle threads that shatter easily. When the mixture reaches the right temperature, add the optional food coloring and flavoring, stirring well.

geologic: having to do with geology, the science of the history of the earth.

(PS) Plate Maps

The U.S. **Geological** Survey has a map of the earth's plates with boundary types. You can look at it here. What do you notice about the edges of the plates?

This Dynamic Planet map 🔍

Slowly pour the hot "liquid rock" onto the baking sheet, starting at the center of the sheet and letting it spread outward.

Let it cool slightly but not completely. Have an adult test the temperature. Make sure it's cool enough to handle.

Wearing food gloves to protect your hands, roll up an edge of your lava. Before it cools completely, it will be easy to bend and push into shapes. Make ridges, trenches, and volcanoes in the lava!

Once it cools completely, your molten rock will be "rock hard," just like real rock! You can eat it, but be careful of your teeth.

TRY THIS: Design and build a Lego city on the greased baking sheet. Make another batch of lava and pour it through the city. What happens to the buildings? What are some precautions a population can take to avoid being damaged by volcanoes or earthquakes?

ACTIVITY

Plate Boundaries

Explore the different types of boundaries and see what happens when the plates move around each other.

Cut a piece of foam paper in half, making the edge jagged instead of smooth. Float your foam pieces in a container of water, which represents the middle and lower mantles, and recreate the movements of the plates.

* How do you simulate a divergent boundary? What do you see?

* Create a convergent boundary. How is this different from a divergent boundary? What happens with the water?

* How do you make a transform boundary? What natural occurrences can result from this boundary?

TRY THIS: Think about some of the landforms around you or those you've seen when you've traveled. What types of boundaries might have formed those landforms?

Fun Fact

Australia continues to move northeast every year, and India continues to push against Asia in a move that formed the Himalayas.

ACTIVITY

Convection Currents

The plates move because of convection currents in the mantle. This is caused by the temperature being hotter in some places than in others. You can see this phenomena with water.

Fill a large container with water and set aside. Make an ice cube in an ice cube tray, adding food coloring to change the color.

Fill a small container that won't float with very hot water and use the food coloring to tint it a different color than the ice cube.

Holding your finger over the opening on the small container, place it on its side in the bottom of the large glass container. At the same time, have a helper place the tinted ice cube in the large container. Release your finger from the mouth of the small container. What happens?

*   Which direction does the colored water from the melting ice cube flow?

*   Which direction does the colored hot water from the smaller container flow?

*   How does the movement of the colored water change?

*   What color is the water when the ice cube has melted?

THINK ABOUT IT: Why did the water with different temperatures move? Think about the properties of cold water versus warm water, and why some objects float and others sink. Use this example to explain convection currents in the mantle.

ACTIVITY

23

Pangaea Puzzle

The earth's continents are shaped like puzzle pieces that can be put together to form one huge continent. One reason scientists discovered this huge continent is because similar fossils were found across the oceans from each other. In this project, you can create a puzzle map to show how the fossil record supports the theory of plate tectonics.

Caution: You must have permission to use the Internet.

Trace every continent from a map of the world and create puzzle pieces out of these continents.

Do some research on the Internet where different types of fossils have been found. Try the key words "fossil evidence map." Add these areas to your puzzle pieces and color code the different kinds of fossils. Create a key to keep track of which colors represent which fossils.

* Where do your puzzle pieces match up according to the fossil key?

* Where do they match up according to shape? Is it the same? Why?

* How does your map support the theory of plate tectonics?

* What other conclusions might early scientists have drawn to explain the placement of the fossils?

THINK ABOUT IT: How do you think the evolution of the earth's surface has affected the development of certain **species** of animals? Can you find any links between certain species that look similar, but live on completely different continents? Maybe those similar creatures have changed through time to have different characteristics—a longer beak, for example. Why would that have happened? How has the breakup of Pangaea influenced the evolution of some creatures?

WORDS TO KNOW

species: a group of plants or animals that are closely related and produce offspring.

ACTIVITY

Chapter 2

EARTHQUAKES

On the evening of March 27, 1964, the earth just east of Anchorage, Alaska, began shaking and moving. For more than three minutes, the ground rocked, buildings swayed, and roads buckled. The surface of the earth was transformed into a dipping, weaving, unpredictable surfboard that people had to struggle to stand upright on.

This earthquake unleashed **avalanches**, underwater **landslides**, ground **fissures**, and enormous waves called **tsunamis**. It was a 9.2-magnitude earthquake, the most powerful earthquake to be recorded in North America. It's the second-most powerful earthquake ever recorded in the world.

ESSENTIAL QUESTION

Are there any benefits to earthquakes? Do they serve a valuable purpose for our planet?

The aftermath was permanent in some cases. Some areas saw the earth raised as high as 30 feet! The coastline was reshaped. There were 11 recorded **aftershocks** that were greater than 6.2 magnitude.

THE STRUCTURE OF THE EARTH

In Chapter One, you learned that the earth isn't simply a solid chunk of rock. Instead, at the very center of the earth is the inner core. Remember, even though the inner core is just a little smaller than the moon, it's made of metal so hot that it's about as hot as the surface of the sun! Surrounding that inner core is the outer core, which is made of melted metal, but just a little less hot. The next layer is the mantle, which is the thickest part of the earth. Even though it's made of rock and not as hot as the cores, it's still hot enough that those rocks are weak and flow in a solid state.

The deeper mantle is hotter but under very high pressure, so it is more dense, stronger, and more solid.

The mantle is similar to hot pavement that's being poured down to make a road—it's kind of thick and solid, but still weak enough to move. This movement is why earthquakes happen.

Sitting on top of the mantle is one final layer of the earth—the crust. The plates contain all of the crust and the upper mantle, which form the lithosphere. The crust and mantle of the lithosphere are cold enough to be brittle and break into plates that shift very, very slowly on the hotter mantle below.

Fun Fact

A whopping 90 percent of the earth's earthquakes and volcanoes happen in the Pacific Ring of Fire.

WHAT'S HAPPENING?

When those plates move toward, away, or alongside each other, earthquakes can happen at their boundaries. In the Pacific Ocean, there's so much earthquake and volcano activity it's called the "Pacific Ring of Fire." It's an active area because there are several plates rubbing up against each other in this area. You can see where the Ring of Fire is located in the picture on the front cover of this book.

PS

Anchorage, Alaska

The 1964 earthquake in Anchorage, Alaska, was the greatest earthquake ever recorded in North America. The earthquake and the resulting tsunamis killed 131 people. Scientists used the event to learn more about plate tectonics and subduction zones. The earthquake was caused by an **oceanic plate** slipping under a **continental plate**. At their convergent boundary, the Pacific Plate lurched northward underneath the North American Plate. You can see footage of the aftermath of the 1964 Anchorage earthquake at this website.

1964 Alaska earthquake 🔍

friction: the force that resists motion between two objects in contact.

WORDS TO KNOW

The motion of plates against each other isn't smooth. The plates don't glide gently—if they did, no earthquakes would result from this motion.

The edges of the plates are rough and uneven, so the plates tend to get caught against each other. The lithosphere, the crust of the earth and the upper mantle, stays in one place as motion continues below because of the weaker, hotter rocks. This creates a huge amount of pent-up energy.

Eventually, the crust can't stay put any longer, and it moves in a sudden jump. That's when you've got an earthquake.

Have you ever tried to open a sealed chip bag by pulling the two sides of the bag away from each other, but it just didn't want to open? So you kept pulling and pulling, applying more and more pressure, when suddenly, BAM! You've applied enough force that the bag suddenly pops open, throwing chips into the air and all over the floor! That's similar to the tension and sudden movement that happens in an earthquake.

When the plates have moved far enough against the resistance of their rough edges, the pressure gets too great, the edges suddenly unstick, and there's sudden, major movement. This is because the force of the movement underground has overcome the **friction** of the rough edges.

WHY DOES THE EARTH SHAKE?

During an earthquake, stored-up energy is released. This energy radiates from that point in all directions, similar to waves rippling on the surface of a pond. The weak areas where this happens are called faults.

Imagine if you broke a dinner plate and glued it back together. The seam where you applied the glue isn't going to be as strong as the solid plate around it. It's going to be weaker. Fault lines are similar to those seams. They are where the crust has been fractured before by the movement of the plates.

Fault lines are weak spots that are likely to be affected by the movement of the plates around them.

Pressure builds up at these fault lines because of the movement of the plates and the mantle beneath them. When the pressure gets too great, the seam can shift or buckle, creating an earthquake.

One big fault line in the United States is the San Andreas Fault, which runs almost the whole length of California. On the western side of the fault, the Pacific Plate is slowly creeping northward. On the eastern side, the North American Plate is slowly sliding southward. There have been several major earthquakes along this fault, including the 1906 earthquake that destroyed San Francisco and killed thousands of people.

Richter scale: a measurement scale scientists use to evaluate the size of earthquakes, especially smaller ones.

seismograph: an instrument that measures the intensity of a seismic wave.

WORDS TO KNOW

HOW BIG IS BIG?

Before the 1930s, it was hard for people to know exactly how large an earthquake was. There was no way to measure them or describe them. And earthquakes can be very, very different from each other. Some just feel like a big truck rumbled down the street. Stronger earthquakes are unmistakable.

Really large earthquakes can cause buildings to fall down and can destroy roads and other structures. They can even create enormous, visible breaks in the earth's surface.

Before the Seismograph

Almost 2,000 years ago, a scientist in China named Zhang Heng invented the earliest instrument known to analyze earthquakes. His instrument looked like an enormous vase, decorated with birds, dragons, turtles, and other creatures. There were eight dragons evenly distributed around the outside, each shaped downward, with their mouths open. Circling the giant instrument were eight frogs placed exactly below each dragon's mouth—each of the frogs' mouths was open, too.

When an earthquake hit, a copper ball inside the instrument began to roll, dropping out of the mouth of one dragon into the mouth of the matching frog below. Based on which frog had the ball, scientists could tell the direction the earthquake came from.

In 1855, an Italian scientist named Luigi Palmieri created U-shaped tubes filled with liquid or mercury that he arranged along compass points. When an earthquake struck, the mercury inside those tubes would move. The movement of the fluid would stop a clock, which recorded the time of the earthquake, and start recording the motion of a float that was riding on the surface of the mercury. Scientists could use those recordings and measurements to determine the time of the earthquake and its intensity and duration.

In the early 1930s, a scientist named Charles Richter designed a scale that would help people identify and measure earthquakes. His scale, called the **Richter scale**, is based on how much the earth moves during an earthquake. A machine called a **seismograph** is used to measure that motion.

The first modern seismograph was created by an English geologist named John Milne. In 1880, working together with scientists in Japan, he invented the pendulum seismograph.

A seismograph works by recording even the smallest vibrations in the earth. The equipment usually has a heavy mass that will resist natural, insignificant jostling or movement of the earth around it. A seismograph is suspended above the ground, often with springs. It has a part that is similar to ballpoint pens suspended over a paper roll on a big drum that slowly turns.

When the ground shakes, the machine itself remains relatively steady because it's on the springs. The pens move with the motion of the earth, drawing a squiggly line on the paper, which can be measured. The larger the earthquake, the larger the squiggly line. That measurement shows scientists the amount of movement of the ground beneath the seismograph. It can also show how long the earthquake lasted. If there are any aftershocks, it will measure those, too.

Fun Fact

The largest recorded earthquake happened in 1960, when the Nazca Plate lurched under the South American Plate to cause a massive earthquake that measured 9.5 on the Richter scale. It was so large, those shock waves traveled around the world for days!

Know Your Richter Scale

Even though we might not hear about an earthquake event on the news every day, that doesn't mean they're not happening. The amount the ground moves is recorded on the scale that Charles Richter designed. The Richter scale shows how people might notice.

Richter scale	Frequency	Observation by people
1	Several million every year!	Small/not felt by people
2	More than 1 million a year	Barely felt by some people
3	More than 100,000 a year	Often felt, but rarely causing damage
4	10,000 to 15,000 a year	Felt by most people in area
5	1,000 to 1,500 a year	Felt by everyone
6	100 to 150 a year	Felt in wider areas
7	10 to 20 a year	Felt across great distances
8	One per year	Felt in extremely large regions
9+	One every 10 to 50 years	At or near total destruction and permanent changes to the ground

The measurements on the Richter scale go from 1 to 10. Each number takes the amount of shaking and increases it by 10 as the numbers go up. Suppose you have an earthquake with a magnitude of 4. The next number up, an earthquake with a magnitude of 5, would mean the earth is shaking 10 times as much as the earthquake with a magnitude of 4.

Imagine a small explosion at a construction site. It might measure a 1 on the Richter scale. People nearby would hear the sound of the explosion, but they might not even feel the ground shake.

As you go up the scale, remember that each higher number increases the intensity of the earthquake by 10 times. An earthquake with a magnitude of 8, for example, releases as much energy as exploding 6 million tons of TNT. Not only will people absolutely feel that explosion, it will also cause massive destruction to buildings and other structures. The good news is that most earthquakes measure less than 2.5 on the Richter scale, so they are rarely even felt at all.

There has never been an earthquake recorded at this magnitude.

This is a huge earthquake. It can be devastating to a very large area, destroying buildings and roads.

This is considered a major earthquake and can result in a lot of serious damage.

Large areas can experience serious damage.

Minor damage

Shaking and rattling

The lower end of this range is usually not felt.

As strong as a small construction site blast

Intensity on the Richter Scale

10+

8.0–9.9

7.0–7.9

6.0–6.9

5.0–5.9

4.0–4.9

2.0–3.9

less than 2

Relative Number of Earthquakes in Each Size Category

A NEW SCALE IN TOWN

For decades, the Richter scale has been the standard for measuring earthquakes. However, this ranking system is limited, because it has a hard time measuring very large earthquakes. Scientists also use a slightly different scale called the **moment magnitude scale** (MMS). The MMS does a better job measuring very large earthquakes, because it has no upper limit. However, there's still a drawback. The MMS scale has trouble measuring smaller earthquakes.

The Richter scale is still used to measure earthquakes less than 3.5, which includes most of the earthquakes around the world. For those mightier quakes, the U.S. Geological Survey turns to the MMS.

U.S. Geological Survey

The U.S. Geological Survey (USGS) is a scientific agency of the United States government. The mission of the USGS is to use scientific methods and tools to study the landscape of the United States and to learn more about the earth. By looking at the country's natural resources, including water, energy, and minerals, and studying the natural disasters that occur each year, the USGS can provide scientific data on the health of its ecosystems and environment, as well as the impacts of climate and changes in land use. The motto of the USGS is "Science for a Changing World."

You can learn more about the USGS at its website.

US geological survey 🔍

THE IMPACT OF EARTHQUAKES

An earthquake doesn't simply shake the ground in a small area. It has a farther reach than just the place where the fault occurs. Imagine throwing a huge rock into the smooth, calm waters of a pool. There's a huge initial splash where the rock plunges into the water. Then waves spread out from around that point. That's how the energy from an earthquake, called seismic waves, travel.

The focus of the earthquake is where the initial event happens— where the energy is released as the plates abruptly move. That's where the biggest damage will happen and where the most people will feel the most movement.

Seismic waves spread out from the focus just as those water waves ripple away from the point where the rock landed in the pool. How far those waves travel from the focus depends on the strength of the force and the type of ground they are passing through. If they're going through loose soil, for instance, the rippling will feel stronger than if the waves are traveling through ground that is hard **bedrock** and less flexible.

Seismic waves can travel for miles and miles and reach a surprising distance from the original event. This how geologists (and seismographs) can study earthquakes from very distant parts of the globe, including uninhabited places.

Fun Fact

The moon has earthquakes, too, called "moonquakes." They're much smaller and less frequent than on Earth.

35

P wave: the primary wave that is generated by an earthquake.

S wave: a secondary wave that is generated by an earthquake. It is a wave shaped like the letter S and travels at a slightly slower rate than a primary wave. Also called a shear wave.

WORDS TO KNOW

ALL WAVES AREN'T THE SAME

There are two types of seismic waves produced by earthquakes. Primary waves, called **P waves**, arrive at the measuring machines first. These are the ones that draw the squiggly lines. Secondary or shear waves, called **S waves**, are considered secondary to the P waves because they travel at a slightly slower rate. S waves arrive at the seismic recording stations after the P waves. The difference in time between the arrival of the P waves and the S waves helps scientists figure out the earthquake's epicenter.

S waves look a little like the letter S as they travel through the earth. They have sort of a rocking, back-and-forth motion, pushing the rocks at a right angle, making the rocks shear. That's why S waves are sometimes called shear waves. P waves move more like an elastic stretching out and then contracting over and over.

The height an S wave reaches as it moves is called the amplitude, and the length of one wave is called the wavelength.

S Waves

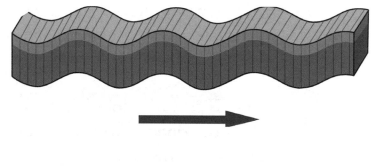

P Waves

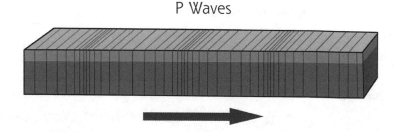

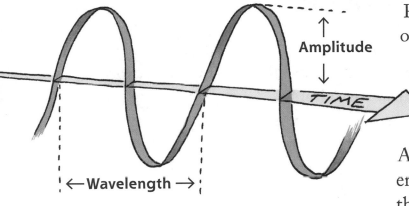

Amplitude

TIME

← Wavelength →

Picture the letter S turned on its side. The height from where the S rests on the ground or line on your paper to the top of that curve is the amplitude. And the measurement of the entire letter on its side is like the wavelength.

The reason P waves travel faster is because they can move through solids, liquids, and gases. S waves can only travel through solids. P waves can get where they're going no matter what type of matter they encounter, but when S waves reach liquids, they fade away. The energy in that S formation can't move easily through liquid.

How fast is fast? P waves travel in the mantle at about 3,355 miles per hour to 17,896 miles per hour! S waves can travel through the Earth's mantle at about 4,474 miles per hour to 9,395 miles per hour.

Why is the difference between the two waves important? Because P and S waves move at different speeds, the

Fun Fact

Shock waves that roll over the surface of the ground during an earthquake can travel far enough upward to disturb the ionosphere, which is the layer of the earth's atmosphere about 50 to 300 miles above the earth's surface.

farther they travel the farther behind the S wave gets. The time lapse between the two waves on a seismograph tells you how far away the earthquake occurred.

IS IT OVER?

The big event of an earthquake isn't the end of all the moving and shaking of the earth. There can be many aftershocks, which are usually smaller earthquakes than the initial event. Depending on the size of the initial earthquake, the aftershocks can sometimes keep occurring during several years! They grow fewer as time goes on—after a big earthquake, there may be several aftershocks, but after about 10 days, there may only be a 10th as many.

Aftershocks happen because of that buildup of pressure.

After the initial earthquake, the pressure along that fault line keeps changing and settling down, but the uneven pressure can continue to trigger shifting rocks and earth along that fault line. Imagine digging a hole in the sand, and the edges of that hole keep sliding down, trying to find a new stable position.

Fun Fact

In ancient Greece, people believed that the god of the sea, Poseidon, caused earthquakes. They believed that when he was angry, he would strike the ground with his trident and create an earthquake.

TSUNAMIS

What if the epicenter of the earthquake isn't right at dry land? What if it's underwater? There are no structures that could be damaged or people living underwater who might get hurt, which is a good thing.

However, there is an entirely different problem that can happen. If there is an earthquake below the ocean, there's still a release of energy. Depending on the type of fault, the land is still moving in some direction. What happens to all that ocean water that's resting on top of that moving land?

Have you ever tried to lie perfectly still in a bathtub of water, and then bent your knees or lifted your legs or arms? What happens? It's impossible to move without moving the surface of the water.

The same thing happens when the earth lurches suddenly, even miles under the surface of the water. All the water gets pushed up and begins moving away from the point of the earthquake. It loses speed as it comes toward land, but something worse happens. It starts to get taller and becomes what's called a tsunami. A tsunami is a monster wave that can travel much farther inland than a typical wave. It's taller, stronger, and far more powerful, too. A tsunami can completely devastate an area.

In 2004, an earthquake just off the coast of Sumatra in the Indian Ocean triggered one of the deadliest natural disasters in recorded history. The earthquake was around a 9.1 on the Richter scale, and lasted an unbelievable 8 to 10 minutes. It was the third largest earthquake ever recorded. And it launched a deadly tsunami.

(PS) Largest Tsunami Ever Recorded

Lituya Bay is an inlet on the northeast shore of the Gulf of Alaska. It's about 7 miles long and about 2 miles wide. In 1958, an earthquake along a fault in the Alaska Panhandle caused about 40 million cubic yards of rock to break free from a mountain lining the northeastern shore.

The rockslide fell about 3,000 feet down into the waters, generating a massive tsunami. The wave surged over land, traveling the entire length of the bay and into the Gulf of Alaska. The force of the wave removed all trees and vegetation up to an elevations as high as 1,720 feet above sea level. Millions of trees were uprooted and swept away by the wave. This is the highest wave that has ever been known—it was taller than the Eiffel Tower!

You can see photos of the land after the wave and read eyewitness accounts of the tsunami.

Largest tsunami ever recorded 🔍

The tsunami traveled across the Indian Ocean to the west, where it hit Indonesia, Sri Lanka, India, and Thailand. Hundreds of thousands of people were killed and huge areas were completely demolished.

Earthquakes can trigger tsunamis much closer to the point of origin, too. On March 11, 2011, a huge 9.0 earthquake struck off the coast of Japan. It started a destructive chain reaction of events. The massive undersea quake sent an enormous tsunami washing over the land. The wave was as high as 133 feet. The wave caused major damage to one of Japan's nuclear power plants, creating a deadly threat of radiation. This was the most destructive earthquake to hit Japan in modern times.

? ESSENTIAL QUESTION

Now it's time to consider and discuss the Essential Question: Are there any benefits to earthquakes? Do they serve a valuable purpose for our planet?

Seismograph

Scientists use seismographs to figure out the strength of earthquakes and to discover the locations of the epicenters. This information can be used to keep people safe. Can you can build your own seismograph that shows a simple version of these critical pieces of equipment?

Your seismograph needs to be able to let a marker make marks on a piece of paper without anyone holding it. How will you accomplish this? One way is to use a box with a strip of paper fed through two slits, one on each side of the box. Dangle a marker so that it hits the paper and records the shaking of the box as the paper moves under it.

* How can you make the marker heavy enough to keep from bouncing off the paper?

* How is this machine similar to seismographs scientists use to measure earthquakes?

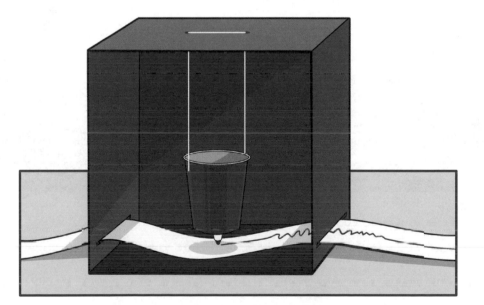

TRY THIS: What are some other designs you can use to create your own seismograph? What supplies work best? How can you test them?

Shake Table

IDEAS FOR SUPPLIES
large, stiff pieces of cardboard of equal size (doubled-up cardboard is stiffer)
✪ *4 or more balls of the same size (small rubber balls or golf balls)*
✪ *large rubber bands* ✪ *building materials* ✪ *ground cover materials*

Sometimes scientists need to know what's going to happen if an earthquake hits an area they're going to study. They also want to know if an area is safe to build on or not, and what types of buildings should be constructed. You can test different types of construction by building a shake table.

One way to build a shake table is to sandwich several balls between two pieces of cardboard and secure it with rubber bands. Can you design a different shake table?

Once you have built a shake table, add ground cover to the top to simulate a building site.

Build cities on top of your shake table out of different building materials. Make predictions about which materials are going to result in the most stable buildings. Test your cities by operating the shake table.

* Were your predictions correct?

* What would you change about each structure to make each stronger?

THINK MORE: How would you build a structure that could stay standing in an earthquake? Would different types of interior supports work? How about changing the shape or the height of the structure? What about the ground cover? Does changing the ground surface make a difference in the way a particular building shape, size, or height survives an earthquake? Sketch your design ideas in your journal and then build models to test your designs.

Tsunami Simulator

IDEAS FOR SUPPLIES

aluminum pans ○ beach balls ○ duct tape ○ large rubber bands

This project will help you see how earthquake motion under water can cause a massive wave many miles away. Make sure you do this activity outside!

Replace the bottom of a deep, rectangular aluminum pan with a large piece of rubber, such as a cut-open, flattened rubber ball. Make sure you make a good seal so your ocean won't leak!

Pour water into the pan. Have a helper hold it while you reach underneath and punch the bottom.

* What happens?

* What do you see the water do?

* Did you hit the rubber bottom in the middle? What happens if you hit it to one side?

TRY THIS: Experiment with different hits, taps, and punches to see if there is a difference in the way the tsunami hits the shore or edges of the pan. Where does the wave's energy come from? How is this similar to an earthquake and a tsunami?

Plate Friction Experiment

This project can get a little messy, so you may want to do it outside! You'll be able to see how the plates grind against each other, building more and more tension and building up energy until they finally release that energy as an earthquake.

Find materials that simulate the grinding together of the plates and use them to demonstrate earthquakes.

Foam blocks work well. Cut them into rectangles without any round edges. What other material will suit your purposes?

Position the blocks so the long ends are lined up against each other, side by side, touching.

Have a friend push one "plate" in the opposite direction you're pushing yours—either toward yours or alongside it, but in a different direction. You should both push firmly, like a backward game of tug-of-war.

* How long will the pressure keep up before one plate buckles to the other?

* What happens when the plates reach the end of their edges?

* Can you imagine how that force creates an earthquake that's felt by people—and even destroys buildings?

* How gently can you each push before the impact becomes noticeable?

TRY THIS: Model the other types of boundaries with new blocks. Can you simulate a convergent boundary and a divergent boundary? What types of natural disasters might be found along those boundaries? Try using blocks made out of different materials. What do these blocks show you about plate movement?

ACTIVITY

Measuring Scale

For a while, the Richter scale was the only measurement of earthquakes. Then came the moment magnitude scale. There are also scales to measure things such as volcanic activity and events such as tornadoes and hurricanes. Creating a scale to measure something for the first time can be difficult. Try it yourself!

What would you like to measure? Find something that doesn't have a scale already. What is something that people experience, but don't have a systematic way to measure or compare events? Maybe you can think of a new way to measure something other than a scale that is currently used. How about temperature, noise levels, or the quality of food?

Once you've decided what you're going to measure, you need to figure out the units you'll use. You can use familiar measurements such as inches, minutes, or degrees or think of a more creative unit.

Make a simple, two-column chart. Label one column "Scale." This is where you will list the numbers of your scale. Label the other column "Observations." This is where you will list the units you decide to use. For example, if you were measuring the temperature according to your cat's behavior, your chart might look like this.

Scale	Observations
1	Fluffy sprawls on the tile floor of the kitchen.
2	Fluffy sleeps on the carpet.
3	Fluffy curls up on the carpet in the sun.
4	Fluffy sleeps beside the heater.

According to your scale, If someone asks you, "How cold Is It?" you could say, "It's a 3 on the Fluffy scale!"

THINK ABOUT IT: Is your first idea for a scale the one you ended up using? Often, scientists revise their ideas and designs to accommodate new discoveries and changes in thinking. What are some other times when you've had to change a design to fit new theories?

Invent a Tool

The first seismograph invented by Zhang Heng was very simple, but very clever. With this project, you will come up with your own way to design an invention.

If you want, you can combine the previous project of coming up with your own measurement scale with this one. Your goal is to create an invention or a tool that can be used to measure an event.

* If you were to tie this in to your project on measuring the temperature based on your cat's behavior, what could you use?

* Think about what actions your cat takes that you used to form your measurement system. How would you measure that?

For example, say you have a white, long-haired cat that sheds. Your tool or instrument might be something that uses that quality as an indicator. For your invention, you might take a picture frame, remove the picture and glass, and secure a piece of black felt over it.

To use your Cat Temperature Gauge, place it in different locations around the house and check your data, or how much hair it collects, at different temperatures. You might find a ton of hair when you place the gauge near the heater when it's cold, for instance.

* What other physical signs can you use to measure your observations?

* How can you create a tool or instrument that will help you collect that physical data?

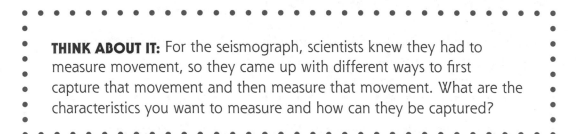

THINK ABOUT IT: For the seismograph, scientists knew they had to measure movement, so they came up with different ways to first capture that movement and then measure that movement. What are the characteristics you want to measure and how can they be captured?

ACTIVITY

Chapter 3

VOLCANOES

You might picture volcanoes as hot, bubbly monsters of mountains, spewing lava, ash, and smoke into the sky, night and day. But most volcanoes are more similar to resting giants that might wake up at any time.

A volcano is a mountain with a hidden secret. Like earthquakes, volcanoes are most common along the places where the earth's plates meet each other and where there are openings in the earth's crust. The volcanoes are mountains or mountain chains that are built up over these weak spots. Beneath them is access to the mantle, which has hot rock sliding around under pressure. Some of this rock at the plate boundary partially melts, either because of the melting temperature or a change in pressure. If the plates shift just right, and if the pressure is too great, the volcano erupts.

? ESSENTIAL QUESTION

What was it like long ago for people who lived near a volcano? How did they explain what was happening when the volcano erupted?

active volcano: a volcano that has erupted in recent recorded time.

dormant volcano: a volcano that is still capable of erupting, but hasn't for a long time.

extinct volcano: a volcano that doesn't have any magma anymore and therefore won't erupt again.

tephra: the debris that is ejected when magma explodes from a volcano, containing materials such as ash, pumice, and small cinders.

pyroclastic flow: the current of tephra that spreads out along the ground from a volcano after an eruption.

density: the mass of something compared to how much space it takes up.

WORDS TO KNOW

Magma is hot, molten rock, usually at about 1,300 to 2,400 degrees Fahrenheit. Since it's lighter than solid rock, it rises up through the crust to the body of the volcano. After enough pressure has built up, the magma can shoot through the volcano and out into the air.

Once the magma makes its way outside the volcano, it is called lava. Lava is slow-moving, but even at its slow pace, there's no stopping it. It can burn everything in its path—trees, homes, and roads.

Even metal cars can be consumed by the searing heat of lava.

The lava slides down the sides of the volcano and slowly cools over time. That erupting and cooling of the melted rock builds up the sides of volcanoes.

If a volcano erupts often, it's called an **active volcano**. Sometimes, though, a volcano will stop erupting for very long time. It can even stop for hundreds of years. These volcanoes are called **dormant volcanoes**. But don't be fooled—just because a volcano is dormant doesn't mean it will never erupt again. This just means it has been a long time since the last eruption. There's probably still magma roiling around inside of it. You can even see steam coming from some dormant volcanoes for years.

When a volcano has been dormant for thousands of years, it's an **extinct volcano**. If a volcano is extinct, that means scientists are sure it is cut off from its magma supply. The chances that it will ever erupt again are very slim.

ANATOMY OF A VOLCANO

When a volcano erupts, there are names for the different parts. You've learned about the magma, the molten rock below the ground, and that the magma is called lava when it flows out of the volcano. **Tephra** is another component of some volcanoes. Tephra consists of all the debris that is ejected when magma explodes from the volcano, such as ash and small cinders. You've seen ashes and cinders if you've ever had a wood fire—it's what's left over when everything has burned.

Tephra rains down to the ground out of the sky. In some cases, tephra can actually flow along the ground, riding on a carpet of hot air. In this case it is called a **pyroclastic flow**. This flow can reach great speeds and be very deadly, depending on the **density** of the current, the rate at which the volcano is exploding, and the slope of the land.

Lava

Pyroclastic flow

Tephra

Magma

Another part of the volcano is the **central conduit**, which is the passage inside the volcano through which magma travels before it erupts. On the sides of the volcano, there may be small tunnels, too, where eruptions can break through and leak out. These are called **flank vents**. The 1980 eruption of Mount St. Helens in Washington was an example of a flank eruption.

TYPES OF VOLCANOS

Although all volcanoes erupt in the same general way, they can look very different. There are three basic shapes that volcanoes take.

When **cinder cone** volcanoes erupt, it looks like a fireworks display. The force of the expanding gases in the magma shoots clots of burning, glowing magma and ash into the air, where they start to harden. Then, the material falls and piles up around the opening of the volcano. As it hardens, it builds up around the vent.

During the course of its eruption, the cinder cone grows into a small, steep-sided volcano.

Cinder cones have short-lived eruptions, and they're found at hotspots, subduction zones, and continental rift zones. An example of a cinder cone volcano is Pilot Butte in Bend, Oregon. It rises nearly 500 feet in the air.

Cinder cone

Another type of volcano is a **shield volcano**. These volcanoes get their name from the way the broad slopes look like a warrior's shield. Typically formed over hot spots, these volcanoes erupt either from the summit or from fissures, or weak spots and openings, along the sides. As the volcano erupts over and over, the slopes keep building up more and more.

Shield volcano

An example of a shield volcano is Mauna Loa in Hawaii. It was built up during the course of about 600,000 years to its current size, which is about 5.6 miles above the sea floor and 80 miles wide at the surface of the ocean. The slope is about 3 to 5 degrees, which is a very gentle slope, as is common with most shield volcanoes.

Fun Fact

The gas in the pyroclastic flow can reach temperatures of up to 1,830 degrees Fahrenheit! The flow itself can reach speeds of up to 450 miles per hour.

Mount Kilauea

Mount Kilauea is a shield volcano located on the Big Island of Hawaii. It has been erupting continuously since 1983! The lava from Mount Kilauea has destroyed more than 200 buildings, including homes and the National Park Visitor Center. Nearby towns and neighborhoods are always on the watch for potential danger. You can see live videos of Mount Kilauea at this website. There are thermal cameras, which record the heat, and cameras that record the light. Why do scientists use both to monitor the volcano?

USGS Hawaiian Volcano Observatory cams 🔍

Stratovolcano

The third type of volcano, the **stratovolcano**, might seem to be the most familiar shape. When you think about a traditional volcano shape, you're probably thinking about a stratovolcano. These volcanoes grow from alternating eruptions of lava and tephra. These substances build up with each eruption, piling on and growing the volcano into a steep cone of different layers. That's why they are called stratovolcanoes, because *strato* means "layers."

An example of a stratovolcano is Mount Rainier in Washington State. It's about 500,000 years old, and lies over a subduction zone. It rises up almost 1½ miles over the surrounding landscape.

PS

Icelandic Volcano

Iceland has about 130 volcanic mountains. In fact, the entire country was formed because of its position on the North Atlantic Ridge, where seismic activity is common. You can watch an erupting volcano here. What do you notice about the rocks? What do you notice about the magma under the rocks? Does this eruption look as you might expect an erupting volcano to look like?

Volcanic eruption in Iceland video 🔍

VOLCANO COUSINS

There are other types of volcanoes that aren't as common. For example, a **lava dome** may form near a stratovolcano. Lava domes are made from lava piling up around a vent.

Mount St. Helens was a dormant stratovolcano, but in March 1980, it experienced an earthquake with a magnitude of 4.2. Seven days later, steam started venting from the volcano. On May 18, a 5.1-magnitude earthquake struck, triggering an eruption that collapsed the north side of the mountain. The magma that erupted prompted a pyroclastic flow that was the largest known debris avalanche in recorded history. It flattened vegetation and buildings across 230 square miles around the mountain.

Today, there is a lava dome building within the summit crater, proving that Mount St. Helens is still active.

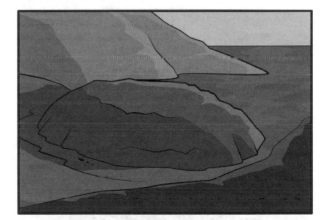

Lava dome

A **caldera volcano** is another type of volcano. Sometimes, if an eruption is extremely large and powerful, it will empty the magma chamber with such force and at such a rapid rate that the insides of the volcano will actually collapse into the empty space that is created. That forms a broad circular depression that is called a caldera.

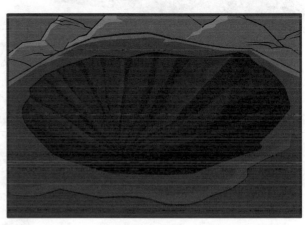

Caldera volcano

WORDS TO KNOW

large igneous province (LIP): a land formation created when hot magma seeps from the ground and flows over a large area, but not classified as a volcano.

mass extinction: when a large number of different species of plants and animals suddenly dies out.

climate: the average weather patterns in an area during a long period of time.

WORDS TO KNOW

An example of a caldera is the Long Valley in California. It's about 2 million years old. The walls of the caldera are 9,800 to 11,500 feet high and the diameter of the mouth is about 10 by 20 miles wide. The amount of caldera substance, or the walls that tumbled into themselves, is about 1½ to 2 miles deep.

There are many places on the planet that have land formations that formed in ways similar to volcanoes, but they're not classified as volcanoes. Called **large igneous provinces (LIPs)**, they are formed when huge volumes of hot magma ooze from the earth and flow out over a very large area. There, it cools and forms different landscapes, including ridges, canyons, and hills. There is an LIP in the United States called the Columbia River Basalt Group. It spreads across the states of Washington and Oregon and parts of Idaho, Nevada, and California.

Fun Fact

Samples taken from some LIPs are the same age as **mass extinctions**, when vast numbers of species have gone extinct. This has led some scientists to question whether the two are related.

Large igneous provinces

PS

Mount St. Helens

The top of Mount St. Helens can be reached only by foot, but you can take a virtual trip to the top at this website! What do you see? What do you think that must have been like at Mount St. Helens when the volcano was erupting?

Mount St. Helens 360 view 🔍

MAJOR VOLCANOES IN HISTORY

The largest volcanic eruption in recorded history took place in 1600 CE at a volcano named Huaynaputina in South America. It was so massive that mudflows were flung to the Pacific Ocean as far as 75 miles away. It was so huge that it impacted the global **climate**. The summers after that eruption were some of the coldest in 500 years!

To this day, a 20-square-mile area west of the mountain remains buried under ash.

Possibly one of the most widely discussed volcanic eruptions in history was in 79 CE, in Pompeii. The people of this Italian town were going about their daily business when the volcano nearby, Mount Vesuvius, erupted suddenly and powerfully. Ash and rocks rained down on the city. Although many people fled, many others were buried in the choking ash.

The eruption lasted two days, and so much ash fell that the entire town was buried. By the time it was over, the town lay under an incredible 13 to 20 feet of ash and stone.

Then came rains, and the ash hardened. The entire buried city was completely forgotten for about 1,700 years! When people finally found the ancient city and excavated it centuries later, they found that the people and their everyday tools and structures were preserved from that fateful day.

Another powerful eruption was Mount Tambora in Indonesia in 1815. In April, it erupted with a power 52,000 times greater than the atomic bomb dropped on Hiroshima in World War II. The fine ash from the eruption remained in the **atmosphere** for three years and affected the entire planet. In both North America and Europe, the ash caused temperatures to drop and resulted in worldwide harvest failures.

PS

Pompeii

You can explore the ruins of Pompeii using Google Maps. What do you think life was like in the town before the volcano hit? What clues can you gather from the ruins on how people lived back then?

Pompeii ruins map 🔍

The year following the eruption of Mount Tambora has been called "The Year Without a Summer."

A massive volcanic eruption occurred at Krakatoa in Indonesia in 1883. This explosion erupted with such force that the sound was heard thousands of miles away. It destroyed about two-thirds of the island, and it also triggered a tsunami that reached wave heights of 140 feet. About 34,000 people lost their lives in that tsunami.

RECENT ERUPTIONS

There have been some major eruptions in the past century. With an adult's permission, do some research on the Internet and at the library to find pictures, video, eye-witness accounts, news articles, and other primary sources about these volcanoes.

Year	Volcano	Location
1912	Katmai	Alaska
1991	Mount Pinatubo	Philippines
2008	Mount Okmok	Alaska
2008	Kasatochi	Alaska
2011	Puyehue-Cordón Caulle	Chile
2015	Calbuco	Chile

Most volcanoes near human civilization are very closely monitored. Scientists can make informed predictions on whether or not there might be an eruption in the near future. They use seismographs to detect earthquakes caused by magma rising into volcanoes.

volcanologist: a scientist who studies volcanoes.

fertile: land that is good for growing crops.

crop: plants grown for food and other uses.

WORDS TO KNOW

How Big is Big?

Scientists use a scale to measure volcanic eruptions just as they use scales to measure earthquakes. The scale to measure volcanic eruptions is called the Volcanic Explosivity Index (VEI). The scale runs from 0 to 8. Like the Richter scale used to measure earthquakes, each number on the VEI is 10 times greater than the one before it.

The release of gases signals changes in a volcano. Another way to monitor a volcano is to measure the shape and size of the volcano to see if it's beginning to bulge, just as Mount St. Helens did before it erupted.

All these indicators can tell scientists if a volcano might be about to blow.

This is not a perfect system. Different volcanoes behave differently, and volcanoes will not act the same way all the time. But **volcanologists** keep making discoveries to improve the science.

LIFE AFTER AN ERUPTION

As you might guess, one of the big dangers from an erupting volcano is the burning hot lava. It can destroy buildings, swallow entire towns, and take lives. There are other dangers from an eruption. The ash that is spread far from the eruption can make people sick, especially if it's thick and heavy. It can coat everything and make breathing a challenge.

The ash can also interfere with aircraft that are trying to fly in the area. Eruptions give off the gases carbon dioxide and sulfur dioxide, which are dangerous to people and animals.

After the danger has passed and the volcano has quieted down, the land around the volcano eventually becomes surprisingly **fertile**. That's because the breakdown of the volcanic rocks creates wonderful soil in which to grow **crops**. People choose to live close to volcanoes to take advantage of this, which potentially puts them in the danger zone.

Earthquakes and volcanoes are two results of the plates moving the earth's crust. In the next chapter, you'll meet other landforms that wouldn't exist without plate tectonics—ridges and trenches.

Fun Fact

The Mount St. Helens eruption measured a 5 on the VEI scale. Krakatoa and Huaynaputina measured a 6, while Tambora was a stunning 7.

? ESSENTIAL QUESTION

Now it's time to consider and discuss the Essential Question:
What was it like long ago for people who lived near a volcano? How did they explain what was happening when the volcano erupted?

Underwater Volcano

IDEAS FOR SUPPLIES

*tea candle or small chunk of wax ○ glass, heat-safe beaker
sand ○ water ○ hot plate or electric burner*

**About 80 percent of the earth's volcanoes occur underwater!
How are these different from volcanoes on land? You've
seen how these help shape the planet—now you can
get a sense of what they look like in action!**

Caution: Ask an adult for help with this project.

If you're using a tea candle, pop the candle itself from the little metal holding container. You don't need the wick.

Place the candle or wax chunk in the bottom of the heat-safe glass beaker. Try to place the piece as close as you can to the very center of the beaker and try not to tip the beaker, so the candle doesn't slide once you've placed it.

Fun Fact

Basalt, one type of rock formed by volcanoes, covers the surface of most terrestrial planets! Mercury, Venus, Mars, and even the moon have dark areas that are made of basalt.

Gently and slowly pour the sand over and around the chunk of wax or candle. Again, you want to be sure you don't shift the location of the wax. Completely cover the wax chuck while keeping the sand lower than one-third of the way up the beaker's sides.

ACTIVITY

Very slowly pour water over the sand until the beaker is about three-quarters full. You want to be sure you cover all of the sand completely, and also allow some extra room for just water on top of that, otherwise you won't see the volcano erupting very clearly. Don't fill the water too close to the top of the beaker, because if it starts bubbling, you don't want it all to spill out and make a mess.

Place the beaker on a burner or hot plate. Have an adult turn on the heat to about medium-high and watch closely.

* What happens?

* What do you see?

* How is this similar to what an underwater volcano looks like?

TRY THIS: How might you simulate an underwater volcano another way? Can you use materials other than hot wax? Can you find ways to make material flow without heating it?

Volcano Art

Although volcanoes can be destructive, scary, and even deadly, they are also an incredible force of nature that inspires awe and can even be beautiful. This project will let you explore the beautiful side of these amazing natural events.

Caution: You'll probably want to do this outside or cover the floor with a lot of protection!

Paint a volcano shape onto a piece of art paper. You can make it any type of volcano you want. Don't paint an eruption—just paint a dormant volcano. Be sure to leave some space at the top of the volcano. You can also add scenery!

Once it's dry, it's time for an eruption! The best colors to use for an eruption are vivid, bright colors. Dip a paintbrush into the paint, stand back from your painting about a foot or two, and flick your brush at the scene. Try different techniques to get the paint onto your paper without touching it.

* How is the paint splatter similar to the erupting lava of a volcano?

* What else can you add to your creation?

PS

Jackson Pollock

Jackson Pollock was an American painter who was well known for his drip painting style. In the early 1940s, he began painting with his canvases laid out on his studio floor, dripping and splattering paint on them, using brushes, sticks, basting syringes, and other tools to make his creations. This was the beginning of the idea of action painting. You can see some of his work here.

Jackson Pollock action painting 🔍

Cake Batter Lava Flow Experiment

IDEAS FOR SUPPLIES
cake mix (the kind that doesn't have pudding mixed in)
❍ large, wide baking sheet or smooth board ❍ timer

The shape, size, and slope of the sides of a volcano can make a big difference in the rate at which the lava flows. You can test the lava flow of different types of volcanoes with this project.

Caution: Do NOT eat any of the cake batter! It will be dirty after you're finished making it flow over the landscape.

Mix water into the cake batter mix, but don't add any other ingredients. Put in enough water to make it thick, like heavy cream, and not too runny or too stiff. Lumps are okay.

Hold your board or baking sheet up on one end about 2 inches. Start a timer. Slowly and steadily, pour the cake batter at the top end of the board. What happens to your lava flow?

When most of the lava reaches the end of the board, stop the timer and record your results. With a ruler, measure the depth of the lava at different spots along the flow. Take note of the shape of the flow.

* Is it a straight flow?

* Does it spread out at the top or toward the bottom?

Use a spatula to scrape the cake batter back into the bowl. Repeat the experiment, this time lifting the baking sheet or board up a couple inches higher. Take the same measurements and compare the results.

* Did the lava flow in a different pattern or depth? Was it faster?

* Did that make a difference in the measurements?

* What happens when you try the experiment a third time with an even steeper slope?

ACTIVITY

Edible Volcano Models

IDEAS FOR SUPPLIES
*margarine or butter ○ marshmallows, miniature or regular size
○ 6 cups puffed rice cereal ○ waxed paper ○ frosting ○ food coloring*

Here's a way to explore the different shapes of volcanoes in a hands-on way. And you get to eat your volcanoes when you're finished!

In a microwave, in a microwave-safe bowl, melt 3 tablespoons of butter and either 4 cups of miniature marshmallows or 40 regular marshmallows for about 2 minutes. Stir, heat for another minute, and stir again.

In a very large bowl, mix together the puffed rice cereal and marshmallow mixture until the cereal is completely coated.

Fun Fact

Yellowstone National Park is an active volcano that has had three magnitude-8 eruptions in the past 2 million years. The last eruption, 640,000 years ago, created the park's huge crater, which is 45 miles across at its widest.

Smooth some butter on your hands to keep the cereal from sticking. Put a big pile of the mixture onto a large piece of waxed paper. You can make one giant volcano out of your mixture, or you can divide it into three sections and make each main volcano shape—stratovolcano, shield volcano, and cinder cone. Don't forget to make a clearly defined crater. After all, this isn't just a mountain—it's a volcano! Use frosting and food coloring to create lava on your volcanoes. How will the different shapes of the volcanoes contribute to the placement of your lava?

THINK MORE: Before eating your volcano creation, tell your friends and family about the kinds of volcanoes and what makes them different from each other.

Chapter 4

RIDGES AND TRENCHES

In Chapter One, you learned about the different kinds of tectonic plate boundaries—divergent, convergent, and transform. These boundaries can be the sites of earthquake and volcanic action, but they can also be the location of land transformation. After all, any time the earth's plates are moving toward or away from each other, something big is bound to happen!

Four basic landforms are created at plate boundaries. We've already talked about the kinds of volcanoes that are formed at plate boundaries. The other three basic landforms are mountain ranges, ocean trenches, and mid-ocean ridges.

? ESSENTIAL QUESTION

Are there places on planet Earth that we have yet to explore? Are there plants and animals that we have yet to find?

anticline: the upward folds in mountains.

syncline: the downward folds in mountains.

asymmetrical: when two sides of something do not match.

WORDS TO KNOW

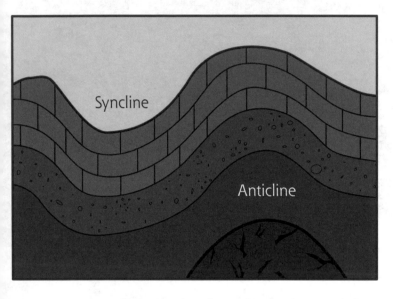

Syncline

Anticline

MOUNTAIN RANGES

When tectonic plates move together, they can force layers of rock to be crumpled. The layers can form two basic features. If the folding of the rocks goes up, it's called an **anticline**. If those rocks fold downward, it's called a **syncline**.

Here's how the folds form. First, sediment accumulates in bodies of water, most importantly in the oceans just off the shore. Rivers often carry sediment and deposit these bits of sand, mud, and pebbles into the sea. Through time, more and more layers of sediment are added. As sediment is deposited, its weight presses down and the pressure on the sediment below compresses it into layers of rock, called sedimentary rock.

> When the plates move, the edges of the continents collide. The thick piles of sedimentary rock are like the bumpers of cars and they crumple.

One example of fold mountains are the great Himalayas, a mountain ridge that runs through Nepal and along India's northern border. They began as sediment in a shallow seabed under an ancient sea.

When the Indo-Australian Plate and the Eurasian Plate moved together about 40 to 50 million years ago, the Himalayas were pushed up and folded. The highest of the Himalayan Mountains, Mount Everest, is 29,029 feet above sea level.

OCEAN TRENCHES

Fun Fact

Ocean trenches are areas of very deep water. They're created at convergent boundaries by subduction, which is one heavier plate sinking under another plate.

At about 4,300 miles long, the Andes Mountains, which run along the west coast of South America, are the longest mountain range on land—they are a long row of volcanoes!

Sometimes the subduction involves a plate carrying a continent that meets a plate carrying oceanic crust. When this happens, the oceanic crust will always subduct, or move beneath, the continental plate, because continental crust is always much lighter. This area is called a continent-ocean boundary, and trenches formed here run along a coastline.

Ocean trenches that are formed along a continental-oceanic boundary are **asymmetrical**. On a trench's outer slope, or the oceanic side, the slope will be far more gentle, about 5 degrees, because the plate bends as it moves downward, under the other plate. But on the inner slope, or the continental side, the trench walls will be much steeper, usually about 10 to 16 degrees. In fact, all trenches are asymmetrical.

The types of rocks found in these ocean trenches are also asymmetrical. The rocks found on the oceanic side include thick sedimentary rocks, while the rocks on the continental side are more likely to have more igneous and metamorphic compositions.

There is an interesting feature around almost all oceanic subduction zones. They have a small hill right before the ocean trench itself. This is called the **outer trench swell**, and it marks the area where the subducting oceanic plate begins to bend and slide beneath the upper plate. This feature is true of all trenches.

OCEAN PLATE MEETS OCEAN PLATE

In many places, ocean trenches form where two plates carrying oceanic crust meet. The great Mariana Trench, which is located in the South Pacific Ocean, is an example of this. It's formed at a convergent boundary, where the mighty Pacific Plate subducts beneath the smaller, less-dense Philippine Plate.

The bottom of the Mariana Trench is the lowest place on the earth.

James Cameron's Dive

James Cameron makes award-winning movies and also explores places in the world that few other people have gone before. In 2012, he descended into the Mariana Trench in a submersible called the *Deepsea Challenger*. He spent three hours at a depth of about 35,756 feet. You can watch an interview with Cameron here. Do you think that exploring the Mariana Trench is a good thing for humanity? Why or why not?

James Cameron Mariana Trench 🔍

Another example of oceanic crust subduction is the Puerto Rico Trench. It's in the Lesser Antilles subduction zone where the Atlantic Ocean meets the Caribbean Sea. The oceanic crust of the huge North American Plate, which carries part of the Atlantic Ocean, subducts beneath the oceanic crust of the Caribbean Plate.

Although there are trenches in every ocean basin, the trenches in the Pacific Ocean are the deepest. They are part of the Ring of Fire that contains the most active volcanoes and earthquake zones in the world.

Fun Fact

The deepest trench in the world is the Mariana Trench. It's about 7 miles deep at its deepest point.

VOLCANIC ARCS

A belt of volcanoes that forms on the top plate above subduction zones is called a **volcanic arc**. The belt forms from the magma that is created at the boundary.

If the upper plate has oceanic crust, the volcanic arc makes islands such as the Aleutian Islands. This chain of islands curls out from the Alaskan Peninsula, sitting above the Aleutian Trench, which marks the boundary where the Pacific Plate subducts beneath the North American Plate.

If the upper plate carries a continent, the volcanic arc is a mountain chain. An example of this is the Andes Mountains in South America.

The Peru-Chile Trench marks the subduction of the Nazca Plate under the South American Plate.

THE GEOLOGY OF TRENCHES

Imagine you are making a pizza, and you want to top it with different kinds of cheese. You might use a big cheese grater to shred a pile of mozzarella. Then you'd use a block of cheddar to add a pile of grated cheddar to your grated mozzarella. Maybe a little Parmesan comes next. How about just a touch of Monterey cheese?

That final pile of different mixes of cheese could be called a *mélange*, which is a French word for "mixture."

At the very bottom of ocean trenches, created by some convergent plate boundaries, is a mélange of rocks, a mixture of different types of rocks all jumbled together. These formations are called **accretionary wedges.** The French word *accrete* means to

Accretionary wedge

"grow or gather over time." These wedges are created as the top plate acts like a bulldozer, scraping rocks off the subducting plate.

Accretionary wedges are mixtures
of different types of rocks. They're called
wedges because that's what they
resemble—triangle wedges.

One angle points downward into the trench. If you take your hands and hold them palms facing down, fingers pointing toward each other, then slide one hand down under the other, you can see the way a triangle starts to form in the angle between them. This same motion results in accretionary wedges. Of course, the wedge you form with your hands is full of air, but accretionary wedges are full of scraped-off bits of rocks.

Fun Fact

Sometimes accretionary wedges are called accretionary prisms because of the way the materials are all mixed up together.

If you were to examine the different rocks in an accretionary wedge, you might find sedimentary rocks from the sea floor, basalts from deep down in the ocean, or bits of continental crust. You would probably even find volcanic material that came from volcanoes on the upper plate. And you'd find that the youngest sediments are at the bottom of the triangle and the oldest are at the flat top of the triangle wedge.

> In most geological structures, the oldest rocks are usually at the bottom and the youngest, or most recent, are at the top.

For example, if you were to dig down into the rock or dirt in your backyard, the most recent material, or the youngest, would be at the top, and the deeper you went, the older the material would be, because it had been there longer.

In the case of an accretionary wedge, the youngest material is at the bottom. That's because as the upper plate slides over the top of the subducting plate, sediments that are scraped off from the subducting plate slide under the accretionary wedge, in sequence, leaving the older rocks on top.

hadopelagic zone: the deepest layer of the ocean.

photosynthesis: the process a plant goes through to make its own food. The plant uses water and carbon dioxide in the presence of sunlight to make oxygen and sugar.

habitat: the natural area where a plant or an animal lives.

organism: any living thing, such as a plant or animal.

adaptation: the physical or behavioral characteristics that help a plant or animal survive.

WORDS TO KNOW

Accretionary Wedges

Different materials make up an accretionary wedge:

› Ocean-floor basalts, which are scraped off the subducting plate

› Sediments that come from the oceanic crust of the subducting plate

› Rocks coming from sources on the over-riding plate, such as volcanic arcs and continental masses

Accretionary wedges can influence the shape of the ocean floor, especially if they're near the mouths of rivers. This is where more deposits are made as the water carries sediment every day. The wedges and sediment can actually start to fill ocean trenches!

If the material continues to accumulate, it can even begin to rise above sea level to create new islands.

LIFE IN THE TRENCHES

Ocean trenches are the very deepest part of the ocean, called the **hadopelagic zone.** With the lack of sunlight and deep, deep water come frigid temperatures. The water temperature is just above freezing. And imagine the intense pressure of all that water pressing down from above! There's more than 1,000 times the pressure that exists on the surface of the ocean! That's a lot of pressure.

The lack of sunlight is another critical characteristic of the deep ocean. All life on the land starts with **photosynthesis**. This is the process green plants use to generate energy. Without the sun, there's no photosynthesis.

It's hard to imagine that creatures can survive in the unique habitat of the deep ocean.

However, there actually is life deep down in these ocean trenches! The **organisms** that live in ocean trenches have evolved during millions of years to live and even thrive in these dark, cold canyons of the sea. They've done this with **adaptations** that can seem strange to people who live on the surface of the earth.

Because of the incredible pressure within the deep ocean trenches, there's no way large animals such as whales could live there. They would be crushed. That is also why humans can't descend past a certain depth. Our bodies haven't evolved to withstand the pressures of deep ocean.

Some of the organisms that live deep down in this high-pressure habitat don't use lungs as other creatures do. They're related to creatures including sea jellies or sea stars, which are commonly known as jellyfish or starfish. These animals are made of water and a jelly-type substance. This is why they aren't crushed by the pressure.

bioluminescence: the ability to create light from a chemical reaction inside an organism's body.

predator: an animal that hunts another animal for food.

prey: an animal hunted by a predator for food.

food chain: a community of animals and plants where each is eaten by another higher up in the chain. Food chains combine into food webs.

WORDS TO KNOW

A human's lungs would be crushed on a descent as deep as this. Human divers have to make all of their vertical descents or ascents very, very slowly, no faster than the rising of air bubbles in water. This slow pace protects the balance of gases in their blood.

Sea creatures that survive in the deep-water, high-pressure habitat of the trenches, however, can move around, up and down, as much as 3,200 feet every day. They can do this with no problem at all because they don't have lungs.

GOT LIGHT?

The deeper you get in a trench, the more pressure there is. In the zones of the trenches that aren't quite as deep as the bottom, there is less pressure, but still no light. Some fish species that reside in this deep, dark area have unique adaptations to make it possible for them to survive the extreme environment.

They produce their own light using **bioluminescence**, in much the same way that fireflies make their own light. Bioluminescent creatures use this light for different purposes. Some might use it to find a mate or repel a **predator**. Others use it to attract **prey**.

Fun Fact

The deepest a human has dived without being in a submersible is 702 feet underwater, done by Herbert Nitsch during a free dive in 2007. The water pressure squeezed his lungs down so they were about the size of oranges! Normally a lung is about the size of a football.

(PS) Deepest Man on Earth

It's important to note that free divers, including Herbert Nitsch, can hold their breath much longer than you could right now. It's never safe for you to force yourself to hold your breath beyond a normal amount! The reason divers are able to do it is because when people are underwater, they experience a diving reflex, which makes their heart rate and metabolism slow down in cold water. For normal people, pulse decreases about 10 to 30 percent, but professional divers can reduce theirs by more than 50 percent!

Another reason is that divers breath in pure oxygen before their dives. The air around us is about 20-percent oxygen. When divers breathe in pure oxygen before a dive, it helps their bodies get rid of carbon dioxide, which becomes toxic if it builds up. Plus, the oxygen protects against brain and tissue damage. If you want to see videos of some of Herbert Nitsch's dives and preparation, look on this website.

Herbert Nitsch 🔍

The anglerfish dangles a little light from an appendage on the top of its head that acts as a fishing rod. It uses the light to attract and lure smaller fish toward its huge jaws. Then, it gobbles up the smaller prey.

NOT MANY RESTAURANTS

Deep in the darkness of the ocean trenches, there's no photosynthesis. Without photosynthesis, there are no plants, which are at the beginning of any **food chains** or food webs. Yet some creatures are still able to live in the unique habitat of the trenches.

marine snow: the organic debris in the ocean that falls to the ocean floor when marine animals die or excrete waste.

nutrients: substances that living things need to live and grow.

chemosynthesis: a process through which organisms get energy from methane instead of the sun.

organic: something that is or was living.

WORDS TO KNOW

Where does their food chain begin? There are two ways organisms in the deep ocean trenches get their food. Think of the layers of the ocean. There are many marine creatures that live higher up in the waters near the surface, such as fish, mammals, plankton, and plants, including seaweed. When those creatures die or excrete waste, some of that drifts down through the depths. It's called **marine snow**, and it's rich in **nutrients**. Some creatures of the deep use this marine snow as a food source.

The second way organisms in the trenches get nutrients is through a chemical process called **chemosynthesis**. This process can be thought of as similar to photosynthesis, but working in a slightly different way. Bacteria in the ocean trenches convert chemical compounds such as methane gases into **organic** nutrients.

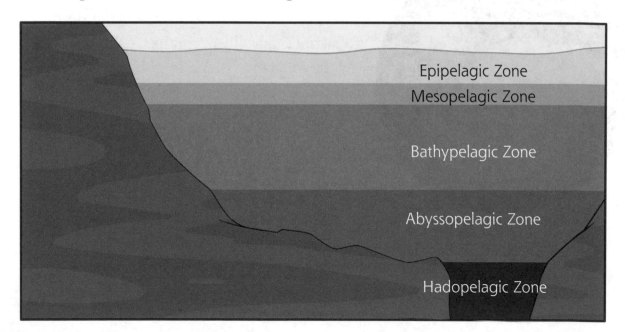

These bacteria form the foundation of a delicate undersea food web.

The food web starts with the bacteria. Then, creatures such as the giant tube worm eat the bacteria, and other organisms feed on the tube worm, and onward up the chain.

Fun Fact

Ocean exploration is fairly new. While exploring an ocean ridge near the Galapagos Islands in 1977, scientists first discovered hydrothermal vents.

Ocean Zones

Here are the five layers of the ocean.

Zone	Nickname	Depth
Epipelagic zone	the Sunlight Zone, because sunlight penetrates into this depth	ocean surface down to about 650 feet
Mesopelagic zone	the Twilight Zone, because the sun struggles to reach this depth	down to 3,300 feet
Bathypelagic zone	the Midnight Zone, because things are dark! A whopping 90 percent of the ocean's water is in this zone.	down to 13,100 feet
Abyssopelagic zone	the Abyss, because it's cold, it's dark, and it's an abyss. At the bottom of this zone is the ocean floor—the only thing deeper is an ocean trench.	down to 19,700 feet
Hadopelagic zone	the Trenches	down to 36,100 feet

Where do the toxic gases converted by the bacteria come from? One source is **hydrothermal vents**. These are fissures in the seabed from which gases are released that can look like spouts of black or white smoke coming out of the floor, curling into the water around it. Clear, hot water can be released, too. The plumes consist of heated water and particles spewing out of the vent, from volcanic activity under the seabed.

Another place the gases can come from is called a cold seep. These are places where the gases seep out of the sea floor and mix with sediments, spreading out over the sea floor.

WHERE NO ONE HAS GONE BEFORE

How do we know so much about an area that's so inhospitable? After all, it's a place that could crush a human's lungs! Until the 1950s, we really didn't know anything about ocean trenches. Almost everyone assumed there was no life there.

Even now, we still don't know everything about what's going on deep in the ocean trenches!

With the invention of equipment called submersibles, it's slowly becoming possible to send unmanned vehicles down into the trenches. But there have been three people who have actually gone down into the Challenger Deep, which is the deepest ocean trench in the world. The Challenger Deep is at the bottom of the Mariana Trench in the Pacific Ocean.

Not So Quiet Deep

When you go completely underwater in a pool, is it totally silent? It's definitely not as easy for a person to hear underwater as it is above the ground, but you can still hear things, and sometimes you can hear things that are pretty far away.

That's what scientists found when they dropped microphones 7 miles into the ocean. There are lots of natural noises that deep in the ocean, such as the sound of earthquakes and even a typhoon that passed overhead. But there were also sounds of propellers and human-created noise.

This discovery is a little troublesome to scientists. Sound from human activities, such as the roar of jet engines or the hum of washing machines, has created almost non-stop noise pollution that is pummeling the planet. Some species of animals are very sensitive to sound, such as the desert kangaroo rats. When they were exposed to loud dune buggy sounds, it created hearing loss that reduced their ability to detect their primary predator, the sidewinder rattlesnake. It took the rats three weeks to recover!

Scientists are keeping a close watch (or listen!) to noise pollution in the ocean to see how it might affect marine animals that use sound to communicate and navigate. You can learn more here and listen to the ocean yourself at this website.

NOAA ocean still noisy 🔍

sphere: a three-dimensional
round shape, like a ball.

rift valley: a long tear formed at
a divergent plate boundary where
the land has moved apart.

WORDS TO KNOW

In 1960, Jacques Piccard and Don
Walsh visited the Challenger Deep.
And in 2012, James Cameron went
down into the trench, too. Cameron's
vehicle was unique because, as it
descended, it spun very slowly to
combat the deep-sea currents and keep it on track. It was shaped
like a **sphere** to help distribute the force of the incredible pressure.
If it were shaped like a square or cylinder, the walls would have
had to be much, much thicker to sustain the pressure.

The submersible was made from a high-tech
foam and was designed to gently compress as
it descended to accommodate the pressure.
The entire unit was 3 inches smaller when
it returned to the surface at the end of
the expedition!

OCEAN RIDGES

The last kind of basic landforms that are
created at plate boundaries are called ocean
ridges. These landforms are located deep on
the ocean floor, almost exactly halfway between
the continents of the planet. Ocean ridges are not similar to the
mountain ranges that you see on land because they are not formed
by collision between plates.

Ridges are interesting because they're geologically active. New
magma rises up to the ocean floor, forms the higher areas called
ridges, then pushes and spreads the two oceanic plates away from
each other. The rocks on the sea floor are youngest at the ridge,
because they're made where the plates diverge—they're new.

As the plates move away from that ridge, more new rocks are formed so that the older rocks are pushed aside. The older rocks cool with age and shrink, becoming more dense and sinking lower. This shrinking and sinking means the ocean floor is lower beyond the ridge.

The ridges slowly continue to spread, forming **rift valleys**. Rift valleys are formed on a divergent plate boundary, between highlands. They're long tears where the land has moved apart, spreading apart the surface. Rift valleys can be on land or under the ocean. The Mid-Atlantic Ridge has large, wide rift valleys on the sea floor. The African Rift Valley is an example of a rift valley on land.

Ridges and trenches are interesting to scientists because they understand that the formations show how continents are able to move. Earth scientists know that ocean ridges show areas where new crust is being formed when the hot magma is released from the mantle and moves upward and outward. That motion carries the continents across the sea. Of course, this motion is incredibly slow, but scientists can still measure it with accurate instruments.

Fun Fact

The rocks that make up the oceanic crust are younger than the earth itself—the crust in ocean basins is less than 200 million years old! That's because the crust is in a constant state of renewal at ocean ridges.

Try This

Hold your hands flat together with your fingers pointed up. Hold your hands over a spout of water, such as a hose or strong drinking fountain. Let the water spurt up through your fingertips. How is this water coming through your hands similar to the magma coming out of the earth? Which water is newer, the stuff running down your hands or the stuff spurting through your fingers?

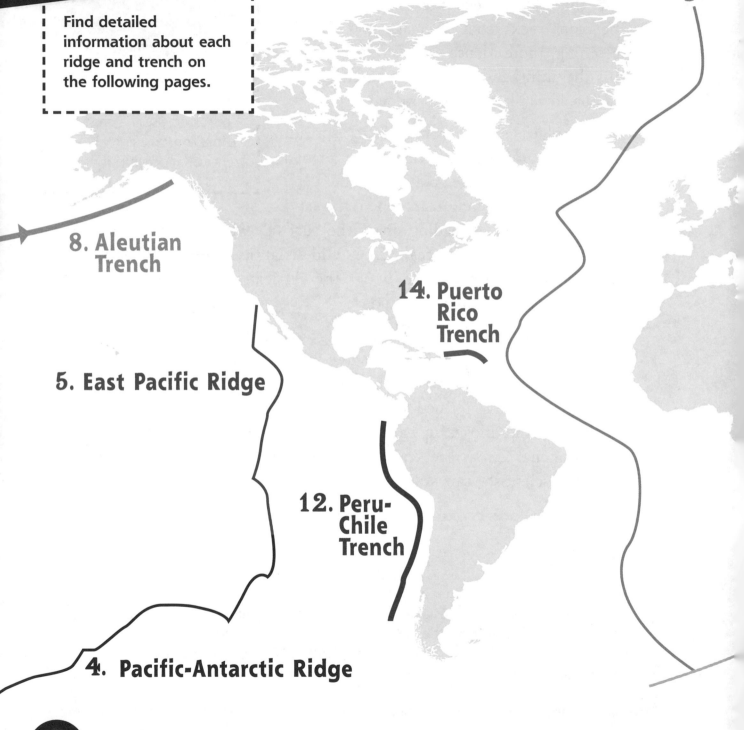

Fun Fact

Find detailed information about each ridge and trench on the following pages.

1. Mid-Atlantic Ridge

8. Aleutian Trench

14. Puerto Rico Trench

5. East Pacific Ridge

12. Peru-Chile Trench

4. Pacific-Antarctic Ridge

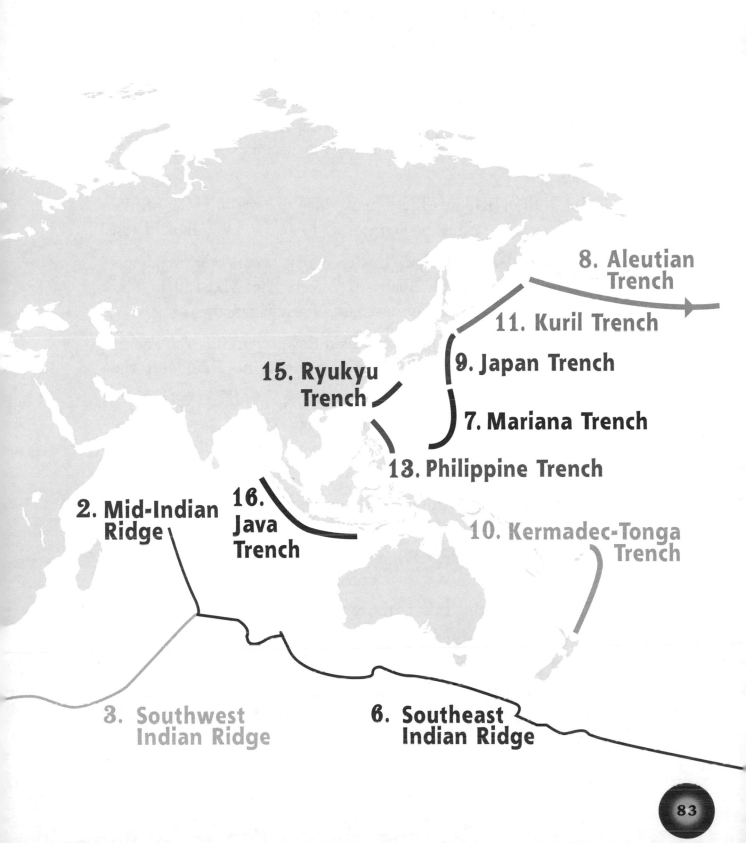

8. **Aleutian Trench**

11. **Kuril Trench**

15. **Ryukyu Trench**

9. **Japan Trench**

7. **Mariana Trench**

13. **Philippine Trench**

2. **Mid-Indian Ridge**

16. **Java Trench**

10. **Kermadec-Tonga Trench**

3. **Southwest Indian Ridge**

6. **Southeast Indian Ridge**

RIDGES AND TRENCHES OF THE WORLD

1. Mid-Atlantic Ridge: The Mid-Atlantic Ridge is about 7,000 miles long. Some of its mountain peaks are so large they reach the surface of the ocean, creating islands—including the huge island of Iceland!

2. Mid-Indian Ridge: The ocean ridge in the middle of the Indian Ocean, separating the African and Australian-Indian Plates.

3. Southwest Indian Ridge: This divergent ocean ridge separates the African and Antarctic Plates. It meets the Mid-Indian and Southeast Indian Ridges off the coast of Madagascar.

4. Pacific-Antarctic Ridge: The ocean ridge separating the Pacific and Antarctic Plates. This ridge joins the Pacific Ridge off the coast of South America.

5. East Pacific Ridge: This ocean ridge marks the boundary between the southern edges of the Pacific and Cocos Islands Plates and the northern edges of the Pacific and Nazca Plates.

6. Southeast Indian Ridge: This divergent ocean ridge separates the Antarctic Plate and the Australian-Indian Plate. The islands of Saint Paul and Amsterdam (the island, not the city!) are part of this ridge.

7. Mariana Trench: This is the world's deepest trench at about 36,000 feet deep. It's located near the Mariana Islands at the convergence of the Pacific Plate and the Philippine Plate.

8. Aleutian Trench: This trench runs from Alaska to the Kamchatka Peninsula. It's formed as the Pacific Plate slides beneath the North American Plate.

9. Japan Trench: Running on the boundary between the Pacific and the Eurasian Plates, this trench is about 28,000 feet long.

10. Kermadec-Tonga Trench: This trench is formed where the Pacific Plate meets the Australian-Indian Plate, just north of New Zealand, and it's about 35,700 feet deep.

11. Kuril Trench: Located just northeast of Japan, this trench is formed from the Pacific Plate sliding under the Eurasian Plate.

12. Peru-Chile Trench: At 3,700 miles, this trench is the world's longest trench. It's located on the boundary between the Nazca Plate and the South American Plate. It's about 26,500 feet deep.

13. Philippine Trench: This trench borders the eastern Philippines. It's formed as the Philippine Plate slides beneath the Eurasian Plate, and it's about 35,580 feet deep.

14. Puerto Rico Trench: This trench is on the boundary between the South American and Caribbean Plates. It's located off the coast of Puerto Rico, and this trench has the deepest point in the Atlantic Ocean. At 27,493 feet, it's not as deep as the Mariana Trench, but it's plenty deep!

15. Ryukyu Trench: This trench marks the boundary between the Philippine Plate and the Eurasian Plate. It's about 24,600 feet deep.

16. Java Trench: This trench holds the deepest point in the Indian Ocean at 24,440 feet. The trench itself is located south of Indonesia between the Australian-Indian Plate and Eurasian Plate.

?

ESSENTIAL QUESTION

Now it's time to consider and discuss the Essential Question: Are there places on planet Earth that we have yet to explore? Are there plants and animals that we have yet to find?

How Deep is Deep?

How deep is a swimming pool compared to the Mariana Trench? Mountain ranges, mid-ocean ridges, and ocean trenches can all be vast landforms that are hard to imagine. By making a poster and framing the scale of these landforms into a scale you use frequently, you can visualize the size more easily.

Choose five familiar landmarks to compare to massive landforms. Here are a few ideas:

* Grand Canyon, more than 6,000 feet deep

* City bus, about 40 feet long

* The height an airplane flies, 28,000 to 35,000 feet

* Statue of Liberty, 305 feet tall

* Deep end of a swimming pool, 10 to 18 feet deep

* Tallest-known tree, a redwood tree named Hyperion, which is about 380 feet tall

Next choose your landforms. Some examples include:

* Mariana Trench, about 36,000 feet

* Mount Everest, about 29,000 feet

* The Sunlight Zone, about 650 feet

* Peru-Chile Trench, about 3,700 miles long

Create a scale that will allow you to accurately draw a massive landform on a piece of poster board. For example, if you were to draw the Mariana Trench, which is 36,000 feet long, and decided on a scale of 1 inch = 1 foot, you'd need a piece of paper 36,000 inches long for your drawing! What is a more reasonable scale? Do your equations on a piece of scratch paper before starting to draw.

Once you decide on a useable scale, figure out how tall you need to draw the landmarks for comparison. How many inches deep would your swimming pool be? The tallest-known tree?

When you have figured out the height of each figure, complete your drawings. How does your drawing of the swimming pool compare to the Mariana Trench? Mount Everest?

TRY THIS: Consider the scale of landforms in different ways, such as time. How long does it take to drive to your grandmother's house compared to how long it would take to drive to the bottom of the Mariana Trench? How many times would you have to drive to school to equal that time?

Landforms Formed by Boundaries

There are many types of landforms that are formed by plates moving at different kinds of boundaries. Use this chart to help keep them straight!

Boundary type	Plate types meeting	Landforms	Example
Convergent	Oceanic-Oceanic	Deep sea trenches, volcanic islands	Mariana Trench, Mariana Islands
Convergent	Oceanic-Continental	Deep sea trenches, volcanoes	Peru-Chile Trench, Andes Mountains volcanoes
Convergent	Continental-Continental	Collisional mountain ranges	Himalayas—Eurasian Plate and the Indian Plate
Divergent	Continental-Continental	Rift valleys	Great African Rift Valley
Divergent	Oceanic-Oceanic	Mid ocean ridge	Mid-Atlantic Ridge

Fold Mountains

The Andes Mountains are examples of fold mountains, called that because of the way the rocks fold against each other instead of breaking or crumbling under the pressure as the two plates are pushed together. You can see what a cross-section of fold mountains might look like with this project.

Roll out one color of clay into a long rectangle, about 18 inches long, 6 or 8 inches wide, and ½ inch thick. If you don't have enough, it's more important to make it longer than wider. Use a plastic knife to trim the edges into a nice, sharp rectangle.

Repeat with several more colors of clay, making them all the same size.

When they are all rolled out, stack them on top of each other, lining them all up neatly.

Now you're ready to create some fold mountains! Using both hands, one on each side of your stack, push gently but steadily toward the middle. Keep your hands braced on the table or desk.

* What happens to your clay mountains?

* What do they look like from the side?

* Which color would be the oldest rock and which would be the newest?

* Can you find the anticlines and synclines?

TRY THIS: Use your clay to explore other types of geology around the world. For instance, how could you use clay to simulate the development of other landforms? How would you use clay to emulate a volcano, or an earthquake, or the motion of a glacier over land?

Ocean Ridge Spreading

With this project, you'll be able to get an idea how the magma rises up to form ridges and spreads out along the sea floor. Use a small box and paper to simulate ocean ridge spreading.

Choose one flat side of the box to represent the sea floor. Make a slit in the middle of this side of the box.

Cut two very long strips of paper no wider than the side of your box. Make each piece the same size.

Starting at the top of each paper, write the numbers 1 through 10, matching where you write the numbers on each piece of paper. Spread the numbers out over the entire length of the papers. Tape the numbers together at the bottom of one paper and the top of the other. Starting at one end, the numbers will run from 1 to 10, until you hit the second paper and the tape, then they'll run from 10 to 1.

Fold your paper at the tape and roll it like a poster, starting from the taped end of the paper. This is your magma! Put your magma inside the box by threading the open edges of the pages up through the slit you made in the box. Pull the paper through the slit.

* What geological action does this represent?

* What is happening to the magma as you slowly pull it through the sea floor?

* What happens with the numbers?

* What do the numbers represent?

Deep Ocean Trench Life Habitat

IDEAS FOR SUPPLIES

large jar ○ construction paper in 5 different colors ○ decorating supplies

Only three people in history have ever traveled to the Challenger Deep, far down in the Mariana Trench. As submersible technology continues to improve, maybe that number will increase. In the meantime, you can make a model of a deep ocean trench habitat.

Choose a large clear jar with a top. Measure the size of your jar from top to bottom. Line up five sheets of construction paper and overlap them evenly so they equal the measurement of the jar. For example, if your jar is 5 inches tall, you'll want to see 1 inch of each piece of paper. Tape them together and trim the extra paper off.

Label each strip with an ocean zone. Decorate each zone with creatures that might live there. With an adult's permission, use the library or the Internet to research the animals that live in each zone.

Once you've added the organisms to each level, tape the layers around the outside of your jar, with the decorated side facing *inward*.

Add more creatures to your ocean zones using clay, hanging figurines, and other artistic creations.

Finally, fill the jar with water and put the lid on. When you look through the jar, you can see the layers of the ocean, and the strange creatures that live in the ocean trenches.

THINK MORE: Why do you think creatures look and behave differently in different ocean zones? What would happen if a creature from one zone were to try to live in a very different layer of the ocean? How long do you think it took different creatures to adapt to life in the environment they live in?

Chapter 5

PLATE SCIENCE HISTORY

The study of plate tectonics has an interesting past. As with many theories in science, not everyone always agreed on it. That's because science relies on proof, or things that can be measured and documented. The movement of the earth's continents millions of years before people arrived on the planet was pretty hard to prove!

Plate tectonics can be called a unifying theory. This kind of theory brings together many ideas and concepts about the subject and ties them together. Think of the parts of an elephant. A person unfamiliar with an elephant who encountered the parts of an elephant—the trunk, rope-like tail, flapping ears, thick legs—might think they were parts of different creatures and completely unrelated. Assembled the correct way, however, the parts make sense. Can you think of other unifying theories?

ESSENTIAL QUESTION

What would happen if scientists accepted the first answer they came to and didn't keep trying to come up with new ideas to explain things and prove them?

Early in the 1900s, scientists tried to explain land formations such as mountains and rifts in different ways. They theorized that while the planet cooled after it was formed, the surface of the earth contracted and wrinkled in a way similar to that of a plump grape wrinkling into a raisin as it dries. The scientists suggested that even the mighty Himalayas, the highest peaks on Earth, were formed because they were forced up in the wrinkling process.

However, the scientists were stumped by a geological mystery. At the top of Mount Everest in the Himalayas, they found limestone. This is a rock found at the bottom of warm, shallow seas. Even more strange, fossilized marine creatures were found in that limestone. How could those tiny sea organisms be at the top of the world's highest mountain range?

WEGENER'S THEORY

In 1912, German geophysicist Alfred Wegener (1880–1930) observed that the shapes of some of the continents looked as though they matched up together, like pieces of a puzzle. He suggested that all the continents were once connected, then broke up and drifted apart. He backed up his idea with geological and fossil evidence. For example, some fossilized plants and animals from the same time period were found in both Africa and across the ocean in South America. Other similar fossils were found in both Europe and North America, and in India and Madagascar.

Fun Fact

On May 25, 2014, 13-year-old Malavath Purna, a girl from India, became the youngest person to ever reach the summit of Everest.

Scaling the Mountain

In the 1920s, an English mountaineer named George Mallory participated in three expeditions to scale Mount Everest, primarily to map the area and to discover whether a route to the summit was possible. On his last attempt, he and his climbing partner disappeared. His body was discovered 75 years later, and the climbing community still doesn't know if he made it to the summit or not.

In 1953, a New Zealand explorer named Edmund Hillary, together with Sherpa Tenzing Norgay, became the first climbers to be known to reach the top of Mount Everest. There were more than 400 people who helped them in the expedition, including 362 porters and 20 guides. There was 10,000 pounds of baggage! Only Hillary and Norgay planned to continue to the top, because of the treacherous conditions and lack of oxygen. When they finally reached the summit, they took photographs for proof, and Norgay left chocolates in the snow as an offering to the mountain. Hillary left a cross from the expedition leader.

Hillary went on exploring the planet, becoming the first person to both summit Everest and reach the North and South Poles. He devoted most of his life to helping the people of Nepal, and because of him, many schools and hospitals were built there. You can see photos of the ascent to the top of Mount Everest here.

Time Hillary Everest 🔍

There was no way to explain how those organisms could have traveled across the oceans that exist there now.

That's why Wegener suggested that these land pieces had once been together, in a massive single continent called Pangaea. There was just one problem—he couldn't quite figure out how the continents had moved. How did they break apart and travel so far from each other?

WORDS TO KNOW

centrifugal force: the outward force on an object moving in a curved path.

meteorological: involving the weather and climate.

jet stream: a high-speed flow of air high in the atmosphere above the Northern Hemisphere that flows from west to east and often brings weather with it.

WORDS TO KNOW

Wegener explored different theories that might explain it. He proposed that as the earth rotated, it created a **centrifugal force**. This is the same force you feel if you spin around really fast on a merry-go-round and you have to hang on so you don't fall off.

Wegener suggested that perhaps Pangaea broke apart and the pieces moved away from each other as the earth rotated. He called this a "pole-fleeing" force, because he said the continent originated near current Antarctica and as it broke apart, the pieces arranged around the equator. Scientists rejected the pole-fleeing theory because they calculated that the amount of force that is generated by the rotation of the earth would never be enough to actually move land pieces the size of the continents.

Wegener also suggested that the gravitational pulls of the sun and moon could have moved the continent pieces, but this idea was also rejected as not possible. Since he could never find any proof to his theory, most people and fellow scientists were critical of his ideas and dismissed them.

HOLMES'S THEORY

As Wegener tried but failed to prove his theory of plate tectonics, a British geologist named Arthur Holmes (1890-1965) dug deeper into the idea that the earth's mantle undergoes thermal convection. Earlier, you learned about convection currents. Convection happens when a gas or liquid is heated or cooled. When it is heated, its density decreases and it rises to the surface. Once there, it cools and sinks again.

Fun Fact

Sometimes, the words *centrifugal* and *centripetal* forces get confused. They both involve circular motion, but centrifugal refers to an object moving away from rotation, as mud flies off a spinning tire, and centripetal force is the force that keeps something in a circular path, such as a satellite orbiting a planet.

Wegener's Map

Alfred Wegener spent much time exploring Greenland. His first expedition was in 1906, when he constructed the first **meteorological** station in Greenland. From there, he launched kits and tethered balloons to make measurements in the Arctic climate zone. His work helped establish the existence of a **jet stream** around the northern half of the globe. Wegener died during his last Greenland expedition in 1930. You can see Wegener's map of Pangaea here.

Wegener's map of Pangaea 🔍

hypothesize: to make a hypothesis, which is a prediction or unproven idea that tries to explain certain facts or observations.

radar: a device that detects objects by bouncing radio waves off them and measuring how long it takes for the waves to return.

physics: the study of physical forces, including matter, energy, and motion.

geologic timescale: the way time is divided up into large blocks to describe the 4.6-billion-year history of the earth.

radioactivity: the emission of a stream of particles or electromagnetic rays.

WORDS TO KNOW

This pattern of rising and falling, of heating and cooling, creates a current.

In 1929, Holmes suggested that a convection current in the mantle might be causing continents to move, much like a conveyor belt moves items along it. His idea was that the pressure upward in the mantle might be enough to break apart the single continent of Pangaea and move those pieces in opposite directions. Although he was hitting on the right idea, people at the time discounted it and didn't pay much attention.

At the same time that Wegener and Holmes were exploring the idea of continental drift, scientists didn't really have a solid theory to explain natural phenomena such as earthquakes and volcanoes, either. In particular, they were trying to link the actions of the sea to the actions of the land. They observed that the volcanoes known at the time were all near the water and they **hypothesized** that this was significant.

PUTTING THE PIECES BACK TOGETHER

All these scientists had little pieces of the idea of plate tectonics, but the pieces just weren't coming together into a unified theory yet. Then, after World War II, scientists had new tools to use— submarines, **radar**, and sonar.

During the war, the way to win battles was to be the first to spot enemy planes, ships, and submarines. Scientists had worked hard to develop technology to detect enemy forces hundreds of miles away, even at night.

Radar and sonar work in a similar way. Radar sends out a radio wave and analyzes that wave after it bounces off any object in the air and returns. Sonar sends out sound waves and makes an analysis on the waves that return after bouncing off an object in air or water. Sound waves travel longer and faster in water that they do in air, so scientists used sonar to detect enemy submarines and ships. Although radar was invented in the 1930s, and sonar earlier, it wasn't until World War II that there was an urgent, pressing need to quickly explore, develop, and refine this technology.

After the war was over, scientists realized they could use sonar and radar technology as a tool to study areas of the planet. Some of these areas, such as the ocean floor, had been out of reach and scientists hadn't been able to study them before.

Arthur Holmes

Arthur Holmes began studying **physics** as a young man in London, but the field of geology really caught his interest, so he switched paths and began pursuing geology. In 1913, before he had even finished his studies, Holmes suggested the first **geologic timescale** based on the concept of **radioactivity**. He proposed that the earth was far older than anyone had imagined, and his initial estimates have become what most scientists agree with even today. Then, in 1930, Alfred Wegener's theory of continental drift caught his interest. Holmes was too late to support Wegener, who had died earlier, and he never did come up with the hard data needed to prove the theory definitively.

In 1960, scientists began mapping the ocean floor. Very quickly, they began to see evidence for the theory of sea-floor spreading and the theory of plate motion. They also discovered the subduction process, and suddenly all the ideas came together to make sense— plate tectonics.

As the scientists learned more about the sea floor, they found a long ridge running down the middle of the Atlantic Ocean, rising above the surrounding floor and running almost parallel to the continental coasts on either side of it. Then, more mid-ocean ridges were found in both the Pacific Ocean and the Indian Ocean.

Scientists thought that this pointed toward something to do with continental drift.

Shortly after that, an American geologist named Harry Hess suggested that those mid-ocean ridges were the result of hot magma pushing up close to the surface of the crust. He expanded on the idea that Arthur Holmes had suggested—a "conveyor belt" approach to continental drift. He called it "sea-floor spreading."

SO CLOSE!

The proof of sea-floor spreading came in 1963, when two British geologists named Fred Vine and Drummond Matthews matched up the topographic map of the Mid-Atlantic Ridge with measurements of bands of magnetism on the sea floor. They found a pattern that suggested that magma was rising at the ridges and cooling, which locked in the magnetic field at that moment. Then, they thought, this material was being pushed away from the ridge in both directions. They found matching measurements of the magnetic field some distance from the crest of the ridge.

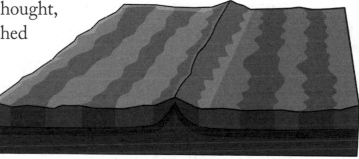

Bands of magnetism represented as stripes

This proved that new crust is continuously being generated at the mid-ocean ridges. It also indicates that the continents aren't aimlessly drifting to their present locations—they are being slowly and steadily moved to those spots, courtesy of the magma conveyor belts that start at the mid-ocean ridges.

And with that, scientists finally had proof of Wegener's original theory, and the science of plate tectonics was created. It was a breakthrough in earth science.

?

ESSENTIAL QUESTION

Now it's time to consider and discuss the Essential Question: What would happen if scientists accepted the first answer they came to and didn't keep trying to come up with new ideas to explain things and prove them?

Theory Game

When Alfred Wegener came up with his theory of continental drift in 1912, people discounted his idea. He's not the only scientist in history who has come up with a theory that was discredited at first, but later proven to be correct. In the early 1500s, an astronomer named Copernicus proposed that the earth and the other planets orbit the sun. This idea was a radical change from the widely accepted theory of the time that the earth lies at the center of the universe. Many people ridiculed the ideas of Copernicus. With this game, you can try to prove your crazy theories.

The goal of the game is to use a unique, original theory to explain something, and then convince others, by using logic or proof, that your theory is valid or possible.

Science is Teamwork

Fred Vine was a PhD student working under Drummond Matthews at Cambridge University. Together, they studied the stripes of magnetism recorded on either side of mid-ocean ridges. They realized that when material from the mantle comes through the ridges, it aligns with the magnetic field as it cools. The material, basalt, is rich in iron, which is strongly magnetic. Older rocks are magnetized in different directions because the plate has been moving and the magnetic field changing over time. Their realization was the observation that Arthur Holmes needed to prove Alfred Wegener's theory about plate tectonics! And it was a great example of how science discoveries and theories are sometimes made. Sometimes, like the push to develop radar and weapon technology, science advances relatively quickly because there's a need. But often, just like the slow-moving plates themselves, discoveries and theories are made with a slow convergence of ideas and evidence. And that's what makes everyone a potential scientist at heart, able to contribute big things and ideas to the world at any time. It's just a group of curious people, observing and asking questions until they find an answer.

Create a stack of cards that everyone will draw from. On each card, write an observation or scientific principle that will become the subject that each player will have to create a theory about and defend to the others. Get ideas for your topics from books, the Internet (get permission from an adult), and your imagination. Here are some fun ideas to get you started:

* an unexplained phenomena such as the Bermuda Triangle

* how early people built structures such as Stonehenge

* how liquid water existed in Earth's early history

* where the weird disappearing/ reappearing dark streaks on Mars come from and why

* why we yawn

* why the sun's atmosphere is so much hotter than its surface

* why 90 percent of people are right-handed

* why in some desert locations rocks move across the desert floor, then change direction and move again

* why synchronous fireflies in the Great Smoky Mountains all flash in unison once a year

* what is behind the Taos Hum, the low-level sound that residents in Taos, New Mexico, have heard for decades

Continues on next page . . .

ACTIVITY

Although his theory was never accepted during his lifetime, Alfred Wegener's work was acknowledged after his death, and honors have been made in his name. Craters on the moon and on Mars were named after him, as well as the asteroid 29227 Wegener and the peninsula where he died in Greenland.

For the first round of this game, everyone represents their own individual team. Everyone draws one card to get assigned a subject and each player develops a theory about this subject.

Set the timer for a decided range for your research and preparation period so everyone has the same amount of time to study and come up with ideas.

After the research period, everyone reassembles. Using the whiteboard or other writing device, each player takes a turn presenting the subject and proposing their theory to explain it.

After everyone has taken their turn, take a vote. You want to choose the two theories that everyone thinks are the most valid. Choose two finalists.

Each finalist then gets access to the box full of supplies. Using models, diagrams, or other methods, each finalist presents an argument for his or her theory, trying to convince the other players that his or her theory is sound and valid.

Players cast their vote for the most compelling, logical theory with the most valid proof, choosing the winner!

Ocean Floor Map

Sonar technology is used to measure and map the ocean's floor, even when it's so deep that there's no way scientists can have a visual look at the surface itself. Sonar stands for Sound and Navigation Ranging, and it measures the sound waves that are sent out and return to the source. With this experiment, you can create a pseudo map to see how it's done.

You'll need a friend, a bouncy ball, and a timer. Imagine that you're on an exploration and you're using the bouncing ball as your "sonar."

Create a chart that will reflect different areas of your mapping area. You'll need to measure time and also write down what you're doing at the time of that measurement. Bounce the ball once, have your friend measure the time it takes for the ball to return to your hand, and write it down. What are your measurements from your position on a chair? On the stairs? From a counter? Think of other places to bounce your sonar.

After you have several measurements, graph them on a piece of graph paper. How would the length of time measurements translate to the distances in a real ocean **topography** map? Plot out the time and draw a line connecting them, and you'll have a simulated topographical map of your imaginary ocean floor!

THINK MORE: What other ways could you measure besides a bouncing ball? What could you do together that would generate different amounts of time measurement?

WORDS TO KNOW

topography: the natural features of the land, such as hills and mountains, especially as they appear on a map.

Centrifugal Force Experiment

IDEAS FOR SUPPLIES
scissors or hole punch ○ *clear plastic cups* ○ *duct tape or electrical tape*
○ *string* ○ *gelatin mix* ○ *water* ○ *marbles*

Although Alfred Wegener was on the right path when he suggested his theory that the continents are moving, he couldn't quite access the right science to prove his theory. Instead, he suggested that the spinning force of the planet caused the continents to break up and drift toward the equator. Although he wasn't correct, it was an interesting and creative suggestion. With this experiment, you can see how centrifugal force works.

> **Caution:** You need a large space to do this project so you don't hit anything.

Make two holes on opposite sides from each other near the rim of several clear plastic cups. You only need one cup to do the project, but if you want to experiment more and see if you can change the results, prepare several cups because you can only use each cup once.

Use the tape to seal around the edges of each hole to prevent the holes from tearing. Tie a string that's a couple feet long to both holes in each cup to form a handle.

Mix up a package of gelatin and pour some into your cup. Pour the extra into the other clear plastic cups. Allow the gelatin to firm up completely. Gently place a marble on top of the gelatin in one of the cups, pushing it down just slightly so it stays in place.

Pick up the end of the string, make sure there is nothing around you at all, and begin swinging the cup around in a full circle!

Spin the cup about 20 times, then let the cup gently stop spinning and take a look inside.

* Where is the marble? Has it moved? Is it in the same place? If so, try swinging the cup harder and faster.

* Where does the marble go when it moves?

* How does this relate to Wegener's theory of how the plates move?

TRY MORE: Think about how you can vary this experiment to test different ideas about centrifugal force. Record your ideas and results in a scientific method worksheet.

Chapter 6

THE FUTURE OF PLATE TECTONICS

As time passes, our planet will continue to change and transform. Earth will experience all the geological events it always has and the plates of the planet will continue their slow movement.

Scientists believe Mount Vesuvius will continue to erupt, perhaps even 40 times during the next 1,000 years! They know there will continue to be earthquakes along the fault lines of the planet. They predict that there will be five to seven earthquakes of magnitude 8 or greater along the San Andreas Fault during the next 1,000 years. And the seas will rise and fall during millions of years as the land changes and new land forms.

? ESSENTIAL QUESTION

What will the future Earth look like?

Scientists estimate the Hudson Bay will decrease by hundreds of feet during the next 10,000 years.

Remember the supercontinent Pangaea? Many scientists hypothesize that as the plates of the planet continue to move, a different supercontinent is going to be built again one day! It won't happen for millions and millions of years, but they are fairly confident it will happen eventually.

Right now, North and South America are moving westward, away from Africa and Europe. There are several proposed scenarios about what could happen in the distant future.

INTROVERSION

In the introversion model, the Mediterranean Sea will vanish 50 million years from now as the continents of Europe and Africa collide. This collision will create a long mountain range. Australia and Indonesia will merge together. As new subduction zones form to the east of North and South America, new mountain chains will be created. Meanwhile, to the south, Antarctica will migrate northward, which will melt all its ice, flood some continents, and result in climate change.

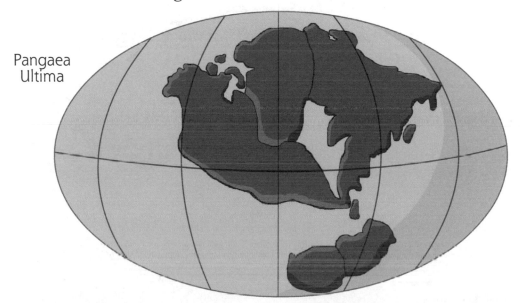

Pangaea Ultima

According to this model, in 100 million years the continents will have gone as far as they can in their current direction and they'll begin to merge. North and South America and Europe/Africa will reverse their movement away from each and begin moving toward each other. In 250 million years, North America and Africa will collide, with South America curling around the southern tip of the African continent, creating a new supercontinent.

Scientists call the supercontinent created
with this model Pangaea Ultima.

EXTROVERSION

In the extroversion model, North and South America will continue their motion across the Pacific Ocean and northward. They'll pass around Siberia and begin to merge with Asia. Antarctica would migrate north, while Africa and Madagascar would also move north across the Indian Ocean, ultimately colliding with Asia. In about 350 million years, the Pacific Ocean would be closed off by the movement of the continents. This model would create a supercontinent called Amasia in the northern hemisphere of the planet.

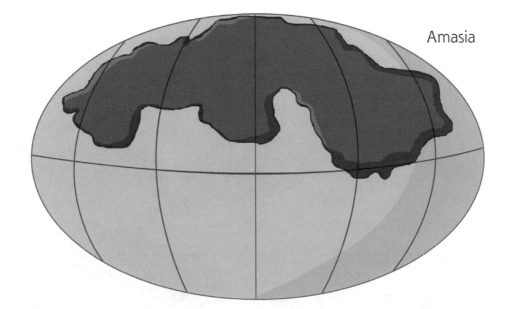

Amasia

Regardless of which model might happen, the impact of a supercontinent would change a lot about the planet. Mountains would be created by the collision of the plates, which would have an impact on the weather patterns. Sea levels would drop. All this would affect the climate, which would change the evolution of animals and plants.

What's more, a supercontinent would act as a giant blanket, insulating the mantle. That would increase the flow of heat under the surface, which would create more volcanoes, creating a warming period for the planet.

IS PLATE TECTONICS THE FINAL ANSWER?

Plate tectonics is an interesting science to study, not only because it helps you understand the world you live on, but because of how the theory itself evolved over time. Do you remember how Wegener proposed it, and no one thought he was right? Then, years later, Holmes helped give Wegener's theory credibility, but there just wasn't proof to make it solid fact. Then, finally, Vine and Matthews came up with the evidence needed.

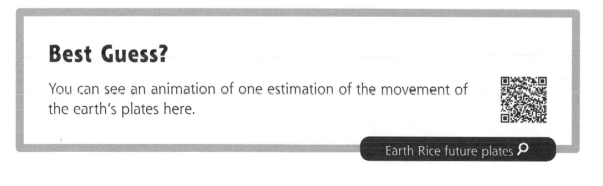

Best Guess?

You can see an animation of one estimation of the movement of the earth's plates here.

Earth Rice future plates 🔍

It's that evolution of proof that makes studying anything in the science fields so interesting. The things that we might think are fact today might very well be proven wrong tomorrow.

For example, people used to believe that the earth is flat. Not anymore! There are many other disproven theories, too, including the way dinosaurs looked. For generations, kids drew dinosaurs looking like giant reptiles, but now scientists believe many were covered with colorful feathers!

Birds With Fur?

If the breakup of Pangaea changed the evolution of some species over time, it's interesting to think about how the merging of the continents far in the future might impact species as we know them today. For instance, what might happen if our continent moved toward the North Pole? What would species that are used to warmer climates have to evolve to adapt? Or what about creatures that live in colder climates, if their land mass moved closer to the warmer equator? The movement of the plates impacts more than just geology—it also impacts plants, animals, and even people.

THE FUTURE OF PLATE TECTONICS

Sometimes, the things that a scientist proposes that turn out not to be true stick with people. They still believe them, even after the ideas have been proven wrong!

In another example, a Harvard psychologist translated a paper by a German scientist in 1901 that said different parts of our tongues have different taste receptors—one part of the tongue could taste sweet things, another part could taste salty things, and so on. But in 1974, this idea was proven to be completely wrong. All parts of the tongue have receptors for all tastes. But people still believe this myth to be true!

And sometimes, there are things that scientists still argue about passionately, such as whether Pluto is a ninth planet or not!

It's very possible and quite likely that scientists will continue to study our planet and discover new things that we didn't know before. They will probably come up with new theories and proof about things we believe today. And who knows? Maybe that scientist will be you!

? ESSENTIAL QUESTION

Now it's time to consider and discuss the Essential Question:
What will the future Earth look like?

Future of the Continents

With this project, you can try to predict the future of our planet in the next 100 million years! You'll need to use the project you created in Chapter One, called "Evolution of the Planet."

Take some time going through each of the evolutionary stages of the continents' motion by flipping through each map. Study the pattern of motion.

* How far did they move?
* With what rotation did they move?
* In what direction did they move?

Go through the maps a second time. This time, use a ruler to measure specific points on the landmasses, such as a unique coastal shape that you'll remember or an oddly shaped peninsula, and record how far each of those spots travel during each stage. Make a chart on your paper to keep track of about six specific points.

After you've gathered enough data from each of your maps, look again at the map for the present day. Place a new piece of plastic on top of that one, and using the data, try to calculate the next possible location for each of your specific points in the future. Consider things such as the time between each point, the distance, and the direction.

When you have your best calculations and estimates, draw the new map for the future, and label it with your predicted time.

* How do you think the earth will be shaped in the future?
* What sort of climate will this new world have?
* How different will your chosen landmasses be?

Future Supercontinent

No one can know for sure what's going to happen in the future. The best scientists can do is make estimations and predictions based on what they know, what they've observed in the past, and make educated guesses. And you can do the same!

Cut out foam representations of each of the continents, and use construction paper to cut out bodies of water to represent the oceans and major seas. Using what you know about plate tectonics, slide the forms around in a way that makes sense to you for the way the earth will look millions of years from now.

Now, think about the impact those changes will have on the planet.

* What will happen to certain animal species, especially those that depend on a certain environment, such as polar bears, or plants that need heat and warmth?

* Will any of those be impacted by your new supercontinent?

* Will prey animals now be accessible to different predators than they would have been before, with the oceans and seas separating them?

Maybe you predict something different from a supercontinent.

* Perhaps you found a way that the continents would slide in a different way, creating separate landmasses?

* Or maybe you realized that a fault would split an existing continent over time?

* Could California become an island in your new model?

* What would happen to the species on that new island?

How about the weather? New mountains could create new weather patterns.

* What can you predict about the climate on your new planet?

* How do you think people and animals would adapt to those changes?

* How would food sources change?

accretionary wedge: a formation made by some rocks being scraped off by converging plate boundaries and gathering into a wedge.

active volcano: a volcano that has erupted in recent recorded time.

adaptation: the physical or behavioral characteristics that help a plant or animal survive.

aftershock: an earthquake that happens after the initial shock.

anticline: the upward folds in mountains.

asymmetrical: when two sides of something do not match.

atmosphere: the mixture of gases surrounding a planet.

avalanche: a massive movement of snow or rocks down a mountain or slope.

basalt: a black, shiny volcanic rock.

bedrock: the layer of solid rock deep underground, under the top layer of soil and loose rock.

bioluminescence: the ability to create light from a chemical reaction inside an organism's body.

caldera volcano: a volcano with a large crater, usually formed by a large eruption that collapses the mouth of the volcano.

central conduit: the passage inside a volcano through which magma travels.

centrifugal force: the outward force on an object moving in a curved path.

chemosynthesis: a process through which organisms get energy from methane instead of the sun.

cinder cone: a small, steep-sided volcano, built by ash and small cinders.

climate: the average weather patterns in an area during a long period of time.

continent: one of the earth's large landmasses, including Africa, Antarctica, Australia, North America, South America, and Asia and Europe.

continental plate: a tectonic plate under a continent.

convection current: the movement of hot air or liquid rising and cold air or liquid sinking.

converge: to come together.

convergent boundary: where two plates come together, forming mountains and volcanoes and causing earthquakes.

Cretaceous Period: a period of time between 142 and 65 million years ago. This is when the earth was quite warm and sea levels were quite high. It is also when the dinosaurs disappeared.

crop: plants grown for food and other uses.

crust: the outer surface of the earth.

dense: when something is tightly packed in its space.

density: the mass of something compared to how much space it takes up.

divergent boundary: where two plates are moving in opposite directions and pulling apart, creating a rift zone. New crust forms at rift zones from the magma pushing through the crust.

dormant volcano: a volcano that is still capable of erupting, but hasn't for a long time.

epicenter: the point on the earth's surface that is directly above the location of an earthquake.

evolve: to change or develop slowly, during long periods of time.

extinct volcano: a volcano that doesn't have any magma anymore and therefore won't erupt again.

fault line: a fracture in the earth's crust. Major fault lines form the boundaries between the tectonic plates.

fertile: land that is good for growing crops.

fissure: a narrow split or crack in rock.

flank vent: a small tunnel on the side of a volcano where an eruption can break through.

focus: the location of the source of an earthquake.

food chain: a community of animals and plants where each is eaten by another higher up in the chain. Food chains combine into food webs.

fossil: the remains or traces of ancient plants or animals left in rock.

friction: the force that resists motion between two objects in contact.

geologic: having to do with geology, the science of the history of the earth.

geologic timescale: the way time is divided up into large blocks to describe the 4.6-billion-year history of the earth.

geologist: a scientist who studies geology, which is the history, structure, and origin of the earth.

geology: the study of the history, structure, and origin of the earth.

geyser: a hot spring under pressure that shoots boiling water into the air.

habitat: the natural area where a plant or an animal lives.

hadopelagic zone: the deepest layer of the ocean.

hotspot: a small area where hot magma rises, usually in the middle of a plate.

hydrothermal vent: a fissure in the sea floor where super-heated fluid comes out.

hypothesize: to make a hypothesis, which is a prediction or unproven idea that tries to explain certain facts or observations.

ice floe: a large piece of ice that floats on water.

igneous rock: rock that forms from cooling magma.

inner core: the innermost layer of the earth, made of super-hot solid metal.

jet stream: a high-speed flow of air high in the atmosphere above the Northern Hemisphere that flows from west to east and often brings weather with it.

Jurassic Period: a period of time between 205 and 142 million years ago. This is when birds and mammals appeared.

landform: a physical feature of the earth's surface, such as a mountain or a valley.

landslide: the sliding down of a mass of earth or rock from a mountain or cliff.

large igneous province (LIP): a land formation created when hot magma seeps from the ground and flows over a large area, but not classified as a volcano.

latitude: imaginary lines around the earth that measure a position on the earth to the north or south of the equator.

longitude: imaginary lines running through the North and South Poles that indicate where you are on the globe.

lava: hot, melted rock that has risen to the surface of the earth.

lava dome: a circular mound formed from the slow piling up of thick lava over a vent in a volcano.

lithosphere: the rigid outer layer of the earth that includes the crust and the upper mantle.

magma: hot, melted rock below the surface of the earth.

magnitude: the measurement of the strength of an earthquake.

mantle: the layer of the earth between the crust and core. The upper mantle, together with the crust, forms the lithosphere.

marine snow: the organic debris in the ocean that falls to the ocean floor when marine animals die or excrete waste.

mass extinction: when a large number of different species of plants and animals suddenly dies out.

metamorphic rock: rock that has been transformed by heat or pressure or both into new rock, while staying solid.

meteorological: involving the weather and climate.

molten: melted by heat to a liquid.

moment magnitude scale: the measurement scale scientists use to evaluate very large earthquakes.

nutrients: substances that living things need to live and grow.

oceanic plate: a tectonic plate under an ocean.

organic: something that is or was living.

organism: any living thing, such as a plant or animal.

outer core: the layer of the earth surrounding the inner core, made of molten metal.

outer trench swell: the small hill right before an ocean trench, marking where the subducting oceanic plate begins to bend and slide under the upper plate.

Paleocene Epoch: a period of time between 65 and 55 million years ago. This is when the mammals and birds evolved into many different forms.

Pangaea: a huge supercontinent that existed about 200 million years ago. It contained all the land on Earth.

perforations: dented lines where something can be easily broken or torn away from the rest of the object.

Permian Period: a period of time between 290 and 248 million years ago. This is when all the continents came together into the supercontinent Pangaea.

photosynthesis: the process a plant goes through to make its own food. The plant uses water and carbon dioxide in the presence of sunlight to make oxygen and sugar.

physics: the study of physical forces, including matter, energy, and motion.

plates: huge, moving sections of the earth's crust.

plate tectonics: the theory that describes how plates in the earth's crust slowly move and interact with each other to produce earthquakes, volcanoes, and mountains.

predator: an animal that hunts another animal for food.

pressure: a force that pushes on an object.

prey: an animal hunted by a predator for food.

P wave: the primary wave that is generated by an earthquake.

pyroclastic flow: the current of tephra that spreads out along the ground from a volcano after an eruption.

radar: a device that detects objects by bouncing radio waves off them and measuring how long it takes for the waves to return.

radioactivity: the emission of a stream of particles or electromagnetic rays.

Richter scale: a measurement scale scientists use to evaluate the size of earthquakes, especially smaller ones.

ridge: the upper part of a range of mountains or a long raised landscape on the ocean floor.

rift: an open space, such as where the crust of the earth is pulled apart.

rift valley: a long tear formed at a divergent plate boundary where the land has moved apart.

rift zone: an area where the crust of the earth is pulled apart.

sediment: bits of rock, sand, or dirt that have been carried to a place by water, wind, or a glacier.

sedimentary rock: rock formed from the compression of sediments, the remains of plants or animals, or from the evaporation of seawater.

seismic wave: the wave of energy that travels outward from an earthquake.

seismograph: an instrument that measures the intensity of a seismic wave.

shield volcano: a broad volcano formed from the flow of runny, non-explosive lava.

species: a group of plants or animals that are closely related and produce offspring.

sphere: a three-dimensional round shape, like a ball.

stratovolcano: a classic cone-shaped volcano with alternating layers of lava flows and more explosive volcanic deposits.

subduction zone: where one tectonic plate slides under another tectonic plate.

S wave: a secondary wave that is generated by an earthquake. It is a wave shaped like the letter S and travels at a slightly slower rate than a primary wave. Also called a shear wave.

syncline: the downward folds in mountains.

tectonic: relating to the earth's crust and the forces acting on it.

tephra: the debris that is ejected when magma explodes from a volcano, containing materials such as ash, pumice, and small cinders.

theory: an idea or set of ideas intended to explain something.

transform boundary: where two plates slide against each other.

trench: a long narrow cut in a landscape.

Triassic Period: a period of time between 248 and 205 million years ago. This is when dinosaurs appeared.

tsunami: an enormous wave formed by a disturbance under the water, such as an earthquake or volcano.

volcanic arc: a belt of volcanoes that forms on the upper plate in subduction zones.

volcanologist: a scientist who studies volcanoes.

Metric Conversions

Use this chart to find the metric equivalents to the English measurements in this book. If you need to know a half measurement, divide by two. If you need to know twice the measurement, multiply by two. How do you find a quarter measurement? How do you find three times the measurement?

English	Metric
1 inch	2.5 centimeters
1 foot	30.5 centimeters
1 yard	0.9 meter
1 mile	1.6 kilometers
1 pound	0.5 kilogram
1 teaspoon	5 milliliters
1 tablespoon	15 milliliters
1 cup	237 milliliters

BOOKS

Earthquakes and Volcanoes, HarperCollins (November 1, 2016)

DK findout!: Volcanoes, DK Children (September 6, 2016)

The World's Worst Earthquakes, John R. Baker, Capstone Press (August 1, 2016)

How Hot is Lava? Kelly Smith, Sterling Children's Books (March 1, 2016)

Ocean Ridges and Trenches, Peter Aleshire, Chelsea House Publications (August 1, 2007)

Lonely Planet Let's Explore…Mountain, Lonely Planet (February 21, 2017)

WEBSITES

U.S. Geological Survey: usgs.gov

Geography and Geology for Kids: kidsgeo.com

PBS map of plate tectonics: pbslearningmedia.org/resource/ess05.sci.ess.earthsys.tectonic/tectonic-plates-earthquakes-and-volcanoes

Geology.com: geology.com

Live Earthquake Map: quakes.globalincidentmap.com

Volcano World: volcano.oregonstate.edu

Volcano Discovery: volcanodiscovery.com/home.html

Live Science: livescience.com/37706-what-is-plate-tectonics.html

RESOURCES

ESSENTIAL QUESTIONS

Introduction: If you were a scientist, how would you try to prove your theory that the continents were once all together as one big continent?

Chapter 1: What would the earth be like if it were still one giant continent? How would things be different? How would they be the same?

Chapter 2: Are there any benefits to earthquakes? Do they serve a valuable purpose for our planet?

Chapter 3: What was it like long ago for people who lived near a volcano? How did they explain what was happening when the volcano erupted?

Chapter 4: Are there places on planet Earth that we have yet to explore? Are there plants and animals that we have yet to find?

Chapter 5: What would happen if scientists accepted the first answer they came to and didn't keep trying to come up with new ideas to explain things and prove them?

Chapter 6: What will the future Earth look like?

QR CODE GLOSSARY

Page 2: awi.de/en/about-us/service/press/ archive/the-copernicus-of-geosciences- alfred-wegener-presented-his-revolutionary- theory-of-continental-drif.html

Page 14: earthquake.usgs.gov/ regional/nca/1906/18april/index.php

Page 14: sfmuseum.net/1906/ew3.html

Page 18: geology.com/pangea.htm

Page 21: pubs.usgs.gov/ imap/2800/TDPfront-screen.pdf

Page 27: usgs.gov/blogs/features/ usgs_top_story/the-1964-great- alaska-earthquake-tsunami

Page 34: usgs.gov

Page 40: geology.com/records/ biggest-tsunami.shtml

Page 51: hvo.wr.usgs.gov/cams

Page 52: youtube.com/ watch?v=RgcMc92CYIE

Page 55: fullscreen360.com/st-helens

Page 56: google.com/maps/d/u/0/ viewer?mid=15850gWF7fOvgJLD 6EQGRmSUYtEk&hl=en_US

Page 62: ibiblio.org/wm/paint/auth/pollock

Page 68: deepseachallenge. com/category/video

Page 75: herbertnitsch.com/ media/videos.html

Page 79: research.noaa.gov/News/ NewsArchive/LatestNews/TabId/684/ ArtMID/1768/ArticleID/11641/Seven- miles-deep-ocean-still-a-noisy-place.aspx

Page 93: content.time.com/time/ photogallery/0,29307,1702756_1516366,00. html

Page 95: visionlearning.com/img/ library/modules/mid65/Image/ VLObject-6115-130725120709.jpg

Page 109: earth.rice.edu/mtpe/ geo/geosphere/topics/plate_ tectonics/plate_future.html